*Love's Witness*

# *Love's Witness*

Five Centuries of Love Poetry by Women

## Edited by Jill Hollis

Carroll & Graf, Inc.
NEW YORK

Carroll & Graf Publishers, Inc.
19 West 21st Street
New York
NY 10010-6805

First published in Great Britain 1993

First Carroll & Graf edition 1993
Reprinted 1996, 1997, 1999

Designed by Jonathan Newdick

The Acknowledgments on pages 349 to 352
constitute an extension to this copyright page.

ISBN 0-7867-0030-0

Printed and bound in the United Kingdom

*To*
*The Monarch of All My Soft Desires*
*The Inspirer of My Thoughts*
*The Charmer of My Bosom*
*The Life of My Soul*
*The Heaven of My Repose*

# CONTENTS

List of Poets and Poems     ix

Foreword     xvii

The Poems     I

Notes on Poets     287

Index of Titles     321

Index of First Lines     329

Acknowledgements     331

# POETS AND POEMS

| | | |
|---|---|---|
| FLEUR ADCOCK | Against Coupling | 107 |
| | Happy Ending | 199 |
| MAYA ANGELOU | Many and More | 278 |
| MARION ANGUS | Invitation | 13 |
| | Mary's Song | 157 |
| ANONYMOUS | Kiss'd Yestreen | 286 |
| MARGARET ATWOOD | Variations on the Word Love | 20 |
| | IS/NOT | 191 |
| | More and more | 267 |
| LADY GRIZEL BAILLIE | Werena My Heart Licht I Wad Dee | 152 |
| JOANNA BAILLIE | To Cupid | 79 |
| MARTHA BAIRD | Do Not Make Things Too Easy | 189 |
| MARY BARBER | Advice To Her Son On Marriage | 167 |
| JANE BARKER | To My Young Lover | 58 |
| PATRICIA BEER | The Faithful Wife | 90 |
| APHRA BEHN | Love's Witness | 1 |
| | To Alexis in Answer to his Poem against Fruition | 38 |
| | Song | 68 |
| | To Lysander | 102 |
| | The Disappointment | 128 |
| | Oh, How the Hand the Lover Ought to Prize | 139 |
| | Angellica's Lament | 245 |
| | Love Arm'd | 248 |
| | The Willing Mistriss | 274 |
| STELLA BENSON | Now I Have Nothing | 94 |
| ANN BERESFORD | The Courtship | 12 |
| LOUISA S. BEVINGTON | Wrestling | 16 |
| SUSANNA BLAMIRE | The Siller Croun | 143 |
| | O Donald! Ye Are Just the Man | 166 |
| | Auld Robin Forbes | 239 |
| MATHILDE BLIND | Once We Played | 42 |
| LILIAN BOWES LYON | The Feather | 194 |
| ANNE BRADSTREET | To My Dear and Loving Husband | 29 |
| | Letter to her Husband Absent Upon Public Employment | 226 |

| EMILY BRONTË | Silent Is The House (extract) | 184 |
| | Love and Friendship | 198 |
| ELIZABETH BARRETT BROWNING | Sonnets from the Portuguese XXXVIII | 11 |
| | XXII | 17 |
| | VI | 46 |
| | XLIII | 185 |
| | V | 188 |
| | XIV | 231 |
| AMELIA JOSEPHINE BURR | A Lynmouth Widow | 141 |
| SOPHIA BURRELL | Chloe and Myra (extract) | 230 |
| MARY CHUDLEIGH | The Wish | 28 |
| | Song | 154 |
| CATHERINE COCKBURN | The Vain Advice | 51 |
| | The Caution | 247 |
| MARY ELIZABETH COLERIDGE | Marriage | 84 |
| | A Moment | 100 |
| | Jealousy | 251 |
| GRACE HAZARD CONKLING | I Will Not Give Thee All My Heart | 161 |
| WENDY COPE | At 3 a.m. | 45 |
| ALICE CORBIN | Love Me At Last | 55 |
| FRANCES CORNFORD | The Avenue | 135 |
| JAYNE CORTEZ | So Long | 266 |
| DINAH MARIA CRAIK | Douglas, Douglas, Tender and True | 142 |
| LORNA CROZIER | Poem for Sigmund | 132 |
| | Last Testaments (extract) | 145 |
| | So This Is Love | 281 |
| NORA E. CUNNINGHAM | Giving | 43 |
| CATHERINE LUCY CZERKAWSKA | Thread | 234 |
| ANN DARR | At Sixteen | 7 |
| MARY CAROLYN DAVIES | Love Song | 15 |
| BABETTE DEUTSCH | Solitude | 174 |
| EMILY DICKINSON | Why Do I Love You, Sir? | 19 |
| | 'Tis Customary As We Part | 209 |
| | My Life Closed Twice | 227 |
| | He Fumbles at Your Soul | 268 |
| SARAH DIXON | The Request of Alexis | 54 |

| | | |
|---|---|---|
| MAURA DOOLEY | No, Go On | 96 |
| | At Les Deux Magots | 207 |
| H.D. | Evadne | 269 |
| DOROTHEA DU BOIS | Song | 6 |
| CAROL ANN DUFFY | Oppenheim's Cup and Saucer | 178 |
| MAUREEN DUFFY | Haikus (extract) | 177 |
| | 'I Am Beset With a Dream of Fair Woman' | 243 |
| LADY CATHERINE DYER | My Dearest Dust | 237 |
| GEORGE ELIOT | How Lisa Loved the King (extract) | 23 |
| | Felix Holt, The Radical (extracts) | 219, 253 |
| 'ELIZA' | To My Husband | 148 |
| ELIZABETH I | On Monsieur's Departure | 24 |
| | When I Was Fair and Young | 187 |
| 'EPHELIA' | To One That Asked Me Why | |
| | I Lov'd J.G. | 18 |
| | To J.G. on the News of his Marriage | 36 |
| | First Farewell to J.G. | 98 |
| | To My Rival | 254 |
| JULIANA HORATIA EWING | Gifts | 228 |
| CATHERINE MARIA FANSHAWE | When Last We Parted | 204 |
| VICKI FEAVER | Coat | 105 |
| ALISON FELL | And Again | 275 |
| MICHAEL FIELD | And On My Eyes Dark Sleep By Night | 5 |
| | Ah Me, If I Grew Sweet To Man | 158 |
| | Second Thoughts | 179 |
| ANN FINCH | A Song | 69 |
| | A Letter to Daphnis | 232 |
| HELEN FOLEY | Touch Wood | 65 |
| KATH FRASER | Song | 176 |
| JEAN GARRIGUE | To Speak Of My Influences | 118 |
| KAREN GERSHON | Uphold Me | 63 |
| | At A Reception | 112 |
| STELLA GIBBONS | The Truce | 71 |
| MARY GILMORE | Eve-Song | 164 |
| LOUISE GLÜCK | Song of Obstacles | 9 |
| | Hesitate to Call | 95 |
| FRANCES GREVILLE | A Prayer for Indifference (extract) | 25 |

| MRS FLEETWOOD HABERGHAM | The Unfortunate Damsel | 22 |
|---|---|---|
| GWEN HARWOOD | The Wine Is Drunk | 192 |
| PHOEBE HESKETH | Love's Advocate | 146 |
| FRANCES HOROVITZ | Loving You | 137 |
| | Women | 175 |
| | Night-piece | 270 |
| | Do You Not Know | 279 |
| HELEN HUNT JACKSON | Two Truths | 85 |
| | Tides | 218 |
| ELIZABETH JENNINGS | First Love | 3 |
| | Thinking of Love | 263 |
| | One Flesh | 284 |
| ESTHER JOHNSON | On Jealousy | 250 |
| ERICA JONG | Parable of the Four-Poster | 186 |
| | Colder | 252 |
| SYLVIA KANTARIS | Body Language | 110 |
| | Not-Loving | 261 |
| | Airing the Chapel | 271 |
| | Stocking Up | 282 |
| FRANCES ANNE KEMBLE | A Petition | 255 |
| ANNE KILLIGREW | Pastoral Dialogue | 76 |
| DORIANNE LAUX | China | 272 |
| SUE LENIER | Finale | 109 |
| CHARLOTTE LENNOX | The Art of Coquetry (extract) | 40 |
| DENISE LEVERTOV | The Sea's Wash In The Hollow of the Heart | 62 |
| | The Quest | 70 |
| | Hymn to Eros | 120 |
| AMY LEVY | On the Threshold | 220 |
| ANNE LINDSAY | Auld Robin Gray | 26 |
| LIZ LOCHHEAD | The Hickie | 257 |
| MARION LOMAX | The Other Woman | 256 |
| AMY LOWELL | Carrefour | 50 |
| | The Bungler | 221 |
| | The Taxi | 225 |
| GWENDOLYN MACEWEN | Open Secrets | 117 |

| | | |
|---|---|---|
| SARAH MAGUIRE | Perfect Timing | 8 |
| | The Fall | 196 |
| | Spilt Milk | 258 |
| MARY DE LA RIVIERE MANLEY | Song | 249 |
| KATHERINE MANSFIELD | Secret Flowers | 61 |
| | The Meeting | 224 |
| 'MARNIA' | Accoutrement | 193 |
| | I Must Be Able To Protect You | 136 |
| | I Want To Love You Very Much | 223 |
| FLORENCE RIPLEY MASTIN | From The Telephone | 113 |
| GERDA MAYER | Narcissus | 111 |
| PHYLLIS MCGINLEY | Midcentury Love Letter | 14 |
| CHARLOTTE MEW | The Farmer's Bride | 82 |
| | Sea Love | 195 |
| ALICE MEYNELL | Renouncement | 44 |
| VIOLA MEYNELL | Sympathy | 235 |
| SUSAN MILES | The Hares | 200 |
| EDNA ST VINCENT MILLAY | Sonnet X | 59 |
| | Sonnet II | 97 |
| | Sonnet XLI | 106 |
| RUTH MILLER | Aspects of Love (extract) | 81 |
| SUSANNA VALENTINE MITCHELL | Of Earthly Love | 64 |
| NAOMI MITCHISON | 'My True Love Hath My Heart' | 233 |
| MARY MONK | Fire Us With Ice, Burn Us With Snow | 121 |
| | Verses Written on her Death-bed at Bath to her Husband in London | 236 |
| LADY MARY WORTLEY MONTAGU | An Answer to a Love-Letter | 34 |
| | To a Lady Making Love | 39 |
| | On the Death of Mrs. Bowes | 88 |
| | Between Your Sheets | 155 |
| | A Man In Love | 156 |
| | The Lover: A Ballad | 162 |
| MRS. B-LL M-RT-N | The Humble Wish | 165 |
| EDITH NESBIT | Villeggiature | 114 |
| | The Kiss | 138 |
| | Appeal | 213 |
| GRACE NICHOLS | Configurations | 273 |

| | | |
|---|---|---|
| SHARON OLDS | The Connoisseuse of Slugs | 133 |
| ROSE O'NEILL | I Made a House of Houselessness | 93 |
| DOROTHY PARKER | Social Note | 35 |
| | Comment | 57 |
| | Unfortunate Coincidence | 115 |
| | Prophetic Soul | 123 |
| | Symphony Recital | 260 |
| KATHERINE PHILIPS | To My Excellent Lucasia, On Our Friendship | 180 |
| | To One Persuading a Lady to Marriage | 242 |
| MARGE PIERCY | Song of the Fucked Duck | 217 |
| LAETITIA PILKINGTON | A Song | 103 |
| SYLVIA PLATH | Love Letter | 74 |
| | Spinster | 108 |
| MARSHA PRESCOD | Women Are Different . . . | 41 |
| | Vicious Circle | 246 |
| KATHLEEN RAINE | Love-poem | 140 |
| ADRIENNE RICH | Two Songs | 126 |
| | My Mouth Hovers Across Your Breasts | 181 |
| MAIMIE A. RICHARDSON | Sonnet | 47 |
| ELIZABETH RIDDELL | The Letter | 48 |
| ANNE RIDLER | At Parting | 229 |
| CORINNE ROOSEVELT ROBINSON | We Who Have Loved | 201 |
| CHRISTINA ROSSETTI | Sonnet | 2 |
| | A Birthday | 72 |
| | Remember | 149 |
| | Echo | 150 |
| | Worth Dying For | 208 |
| ELIZABETH SINGER ROWE | Upon the Death of her Husband (extract) | 151 |
| CAROL RUMENS | Double Bed | 168 |
| MARTHA SANSOM | To my Heavenly Charmer | 122 |
| | Clio (extract) | 244 |
| MARY SAVAGE | Letter to Miss E.B. on Marriage (extract) | 86 |
| ANNA SAWYER | Lines, Written on Seeing My Husband's Picture | 30 |
| LADY JOHN SCOTT | Ettrick | 238 |
| ANNE SEXTON | I Remember | 67 |
| | From the Garden | 116 |

| MARY WOLLSTONECRAFT SHELLEY | Stanzas | 4 |
| --- | --- | --- |
| PENELOPE SHUTTLE | Passion (extract) | 124 |
| | The Old Man | 134 |
| ELIZABETH SIDDAL | Dead Love | 197 |
| EDITH SITWELL | Heart and Mind | 60 |
| STEVIE SMITH | Infelice | 214 |
| | Freddy | 240 |
| | Conviction (iv) | 265 |
| | Autumn | 285 |
| KATHLEEN SPIVACK | love u.s.a. | 182 |
| MARGARET STANLEY-WRENCH | The Storm | 222 |
| ANNE STEVENSON | Sous-entendu | 241 |
| MARION STROBEL | Encounter | 202 |
| JAN STRUTHER | Freedom | 104 |
| MURIEL STUART | In the Orchard | 210 |
| MAY SWENSON | He That None Can Capture | 276 |
| ELIZABETH TAYLOR | Song | 37 |
| SARA TEASDALE | I Would Live In Your Love | 66 |
| | The Gift | 99 |
| | The Look | 101 |
| | Those Who Love | 144 |
| | The Flight | 206 |
| LILY THICKNESSE | Siena | 52 |
| ELIZABETH THOMAS | Remedia Amoris | 56 |
| | The forsaken WIFE | 92 |
| | To Colindra | 212 |
| ELIZABETH TOLLET | On Loving Once and Loving Often | 91 |
| ROSEMARY TONKS | Story of a Hotel Room | 259 |
| ELIZABETH TREFUSIS | A Valentine (extract from) | 77 |
| ESTHER VANHOMRIGH | Hail, Blushing Goddess Spring! | 264 |
| JUDITH VIORST | The Honeymoon is Over | 89 |
| EDA LOU WALTON | In Recompense | 205 |
| MAY THIELGAARD WATTS | Vision | 73 |
| MARY WEBB | Why? | 53 |
| ANNE WHARTON | Song | 215 |

| | | |
|---|---|---|
| EDITH WHARTON | The Mortal Lease | 10 |
| ANNA WICKHAM | The Slighted Lady | 32 |
| | Paradox | 190 |
| | The Fired Pot | 261 |
| ELLA WHEELER WILCOX | Attraction | 125 |
| | The Way of It | 216 |
| | Friendship After Love | 280 |
| SARAH WILLIAMS | Youth and Maidenhood (extract) | 159 |
| ELIZABETH WILMOT | Song | 160 |
| SHEILA WINGFIELD | Winter | 147 |
| JUDITH WRIGHT | Sonnet for Christmas | 283 |
| MEHETABEL WRIGHT | The Disappointed Wife | 170 |
| LADY MARY WROTH | Cupid Lost | 78 |
| | Song | 80 |
| | Urania (extract) | 277 |

# FOREWORD

This book has emerged out of a long-standing liking for love poetry and disappointment at the often tiny representation of women's contributions in most anthologies.

I have restricted my selection to poems written originally in the English language. Deciding how to organise the poems was vexing. I did not want to use a strictly thematic arrangement (a whole section of poems on, for example, parting or bereavement did not seem a particularly interesting way to present the work), but I did want to reproduce for the reader some of the delight I had had in reading for the book. Sometimes this derived from recognising startlingly similar feelings or opinions about love being expressed by women writing hundreds of years apart. On other occasions it was the contrast between the reactions and emotions described by women before and since they have become relatively free to live and love according to their own desires that was striking. So I have tried to produce a sequence or mixture in which the poems can (as they should) be read entirely independently of one another, but with informal clusters or pairs of poems where their mood or subject matter seemed complementary. I hope these juxtapositions will be agreeable rather than distracting. Ultimately the most important thing is that the poems should be allowed to speak for themselves and be appreciated for the fine and extensive body of work they represent.

I should like to thank those copyright holders whose generosity has allowed this book to contain a good proportion of modern material, the staff of the London Library and the Poetry Library for their help, Nick Robinson for deciding to publish the book and my husband, Ian Cameron, whose constant encouragement and willingness to 'carry' our business allowed me to indulge myself.

J.H.

# LOVE'S WITNESS

Slight unpremeditated Words are borne
    By every common Wind into the Air;
Carelessly utter'd, die as soon as born,
    And in one instant give both Hope and Fear:
Breathing all Contraries with the same Wind
According to the Caprice of the Mind.

But *Billetdoux* are constant Witnesses,
    Substantial Records to Eternity;
Just Evidences, who the Truth confess,
    On which the Lover safely may rely;
They're serious Thoughts, digested and resolv'd;
And last, when Words are into Clouds devolv'd.

*Aphra Behn (1640-89)*

# SONNET

I wish I could remember that first day,
First hour, first moment of your meeting me,
If bright or dim the season, it might be
Summer or Winter for aught that I can say;
So unrecorded did it slip away,
So blind was I to see and to foresee,
So dull to mark the budding of my tree
That would not blossom yet for many a May.
If only I could recollect it, such
A day of days! I let it come and go
As traceless as a thaw of bygone snow;
It seemed to mean so little, meant so much;
If only now I could recall that touch,
First touch of hand in hand.—Did one but know!

*Christina Rossetti (1830-94)*

# FIRST LOVE

A fist of red fire, a flower
Opening in the sun. A kind of peace
Taking over at last, and then the quick release.

*Elizabeth Jennings (b.1926)*

## STANZAS

Oh, come to me in dreams, my love!
   I will not ask a dearer bliss;
Come with the starry beams, my love,
   And press mine eyelids with thy kiss.

'Twas thus, as ancient fables tell,
   Love visited a Grecian maid,
Till she disturbed the sacred spell,
   And woke to find her hopes betrayed.

But gentle sleep shall veil my sight,
   And Psyche's lamp shall darkling be,
When, in the visions of the night,
   Thou dost renew thy vows to me.

Then come to me in dreams, my love,
   I will not ask a dearer bliss;
Come with the starry beams, my love,
   And press mine eyelids with thy kiss.

*Mary Wollstonecraft Shelley (1797-1851)*

## AND ON MY EYES DARK
## SLEEP BY NIGHT

Come, dark-eyed Sleep, thou child of Night,
Give me thy dreams, thy lies;
Lead through the horny portal white
The pleasure day denies.

O bring the kiss I could not take
From lips that would not give;
Bring me the heart I could not break,
The bliss for which I live.

I care not if I slumber blest
By fond delusion; nay,
Put me on Phaon's lips to rest,
And cheat the cruel day!

*Michael Field (1846-1914 & 1862-1913)*

# SONG

A Scholar first my Love implor'd,
And then an empty, titled Lord;
The Pedant talk'd in lofty Strains;
Alas! his Lordship wanted Brains:
I list'ned not, to one or t'other,
But straight referr'd them to my Mother.

A Poet next my Love assail'd,
A Lawyer hop'd to have prevail'd;
The Bard too much approv'd himself,
The Lawyer thirsted after Pelf:
I list'ned not, to one or t'other,
But still referr'd them to my Mother.

An Officer my Heart wou'd storm,
A Miser, sought me too, in Form;
But *Mars* was over-free and bold,
The Miser's Heart was in his Gold:
I list'ned not, to one or t'other,
Referring still unto my Mother.

And after them, some twenty more,
Successless were, as those before;
When *Damon*, lovely *Damon*, came!
Our Hearts strait felt a mutual Flame;
I vow'd I'd have him, and no other,
Without referring, to my Mother.

*Dorothea Du Bois* (1728-74)

# AT SIXTEEN

We come now to the space which is boy-shaped.
It has always been there, filled or unfilled.
*Come ride with me on my motor-cycle, we'll do*
*the whole mile-square by moonlight* and we rode,
I clinging to that boy shape with all the girl
shape I was, and the moon made shadows of us
on the corn rows, and we scared ourselves on
the corners, and laughed as loud as we dared
and swung on home before the night could get us.
In the wane of that same moon, he raced the mile alone
and struck an old car parked without its lights
and the night got him, and the moon had to shine
a great many nights before I was sure it wouldn't
get me too. We had been little kids together,
sitting flat out in my sand box, making pies.
We practised kissing in the alley behind his house
and mine. I can still hear the little lights
in his voice that made my nipples stand out straight.


*Ann Darr*

# PERFECT TIMING

The night I fell in love with you I lost my watch:
stripping off at the sea's edge, it fell into the dark
as I swam out into a night thick with stars,
with fishermen calling from one lit boat to another
of their catches and harbours, leaving for the dawn.
Imagine it now, plunged deep in cool sand, still hidden
years later, grains ticking over it one by one—
as your hands slide into me and I move to their pulse.

*Sarah Maguire (b.1957)*

# SONG OF OBSTACLES

When my lover touches me, what I feel in my body
is like the first movement of a glacier over the earth,
as the ice shifts, dislodging great boulders, hills
of solemn rock: so, in the forests, the uprooted trees
become a sea of disconnected limbs—
And, where there are cities, these dissolve too,
the sighing gardens, all the young girls
eating chocolates in the courtyard, slowly
scattering the colored foil: then, where the city was,
the ore, the unearthed mysteries: so I see
that ice is more powerful than rock, than mere resistance—

Then for us, in its path, time doesn't pass,
not even an hour.

*Louise Glück (b.1943)*

# THE MORTAL LEASE

Yet for one rounded moment I will be
No more to you than what my lips may give,
And in the circle of your kisses live
As in some island of a storm-blown sea,
Where the cold surges of infinity
Upon the outward reefs unheeded grieve,
And the loud murmur of our blood shall weave
Primeval silences round you and me.

If in that moment we are all we are,
We live enough. Let this for all requite.
Do I not know, some wingèd things from far
Are borne along illimitable night
To dance their lives out in a single flight
Between the moonrise and the setting star?

*Edith Wharton (1862-1937)*

# SONNET FROM THE PORTUGUESE
## XXXVIII

First time he kissed me, he but only kissed
The fingers of this hand wherewith I write,
And ever since it grew more clean and white, . .
Slow to world-greetings . . quick with its "Oh, list,"
When the angels speak. A ring of amethyst
I could not wear here plainer to my sight,
Than that first kiss. The second passed in height
The first, and sought the forehead, and half missed,
Half falling on the hair. O beyond meed!
That was the chrism of love, which love's own crown,
With sanctifying sweetness, did precede.
The third, upon my lips, was folded down
In perfect, purple state! since when, indeed,
I have been proud and said, "My Love, my own."

*Elizabeth Barrett Browning (1806-61)*

# THE COURTSHIP

I am curiously stirred
by the landscape
as I wait lazily for
my lover
lazily in the hot sun

no hurry
life goes on
time to admire
my long thin arms
they blend with
the long thin grass
their frailty is deceptive
my lover will not be the first
to know their strength

strange to consider
how small he always is
true, he moves gracefully
but never quick enough

when he is joined to me
too absorbed to notice
my knife-like grip
I will eat him inch by inch
I'll not need another meal for hours

afterwards I will sit quietly
under the exotic leaves
raising my arms again
as if praying.

*Ann Beresford (b.1919)*

# INVITATION

Lad, come kiss me
    Whaur the twa burns rin.
Am I no' sweet as honey,
    Wild as gouden whin,

Slim as the rowan,
    Lips like berries reid,
Fey as siller mune-floo'er
    That sprang frae fairy seed?

Luve, come clasp me
    Whaur the twa burns rin,—
A' but the white soul o' me
    That ye can never win.

*Marion Angus (1866-1946)*

# MIDCENTURY LOVE LETTER

Stay near me. Speak my name. Oh, do not wander
By a thought's span, heart's impulse, from the light
We kindle here. You are my sole defender
(As I am yours) in this precipitous night,
Which over earth, till common landmarks alter,
Is falling, without stars, and bitter cold.
We two have but our burning selves for shelter.
Huddle against me. Give me your hand to hold.

So might two climbers lost in mountain weather
On a high slope and taken by the storm,
Desperate in the darkness, cling together
Under one cloak and breathe each other warm.
Stay near me. Spirit, perishable as bone,
In no such winter can survive alone.

*Phyllis McGinley (1905-78)*

# LOVE SONG

There is a strong wall about me to protect me:
It is built of the words you have said to me.

There are swords about me to keep me safe:
They are the kisses of your lips.

Before me goes a shield to guard me from harm:
It is the shadow of your arms between me and danger.

All the wishes of my mind know your name,
And the white desires of my heart
They are acquainted with you.
The cry of my body for completeness,
That is a cry to you.
My blood beats out your name to me, unceasing, pitiless
Your name, your name.

*Mary Carolyn Davies (late 19th / early 20th century)*

# WRESTLING

Our oneness is the wrestlers', fierce and close,
    Thrusting and thrust;
One life in dual effort for one prize,—
    We fight, and must;
For soul with soul does battle evermore
    Till love be trust.

Our distance is love's severance; sense divides,
    Each is but each;
Never the very hidden spirit of thee
    My life doth reach;
Twain! since love athwart the gulf that needs
    Kisses and speech.

Ah! wrestle closelier! we draw nearer so
    Than any bliss
Can bring twain souls who would be whole and one,
    Too near to kiss:
To be one thought, one voice before we die,—
    Wrestle for this.

*Louisa S. Bevington (b.1845)*

# SONNET FROM THE PORTUGUESE XXII

When our two souls stand up erect and strong,
Face to face, silent, drawing nigh and nigher,
Until the lengthening wings break into fire
At either curvèd point,—what bitter wrong
Can the earth do to us, that we should not long
Be here contented? Think. In mounting higher,
The angels would press us on and aspire
To drop some golden orb of perfect song
Into our deep, dear silence. Let us stay
Rather on earth. Belovèd,—where the unfit
Contrarious moods of men recoil away
And isolate pure spirits, and permit
A place to stand and love in for a day,
With darkness and the death-hour rounding it.

*Elizabeth Barrett Browning (1806-61)*

## TO ONE THAT ASKED ME
## WHY I LOV'D J.G.


Why do I love? Go, ask the Glorious Sun
Why every day it round the world doth run;
Ask *Thames* and *Tiber*, why they Ebb and Flow:
Ask Damask Roses why in *June* they blow:
Ask Ice and Hail, the reason, why they're Cold:
Decaying Beauties, why they will grow Old
They'll tell thee, Fate, that every thing doth move,
Inforces them to this, and me to Love.
There is no Reason for our Love or Hate;
'Tis irresistable, as Death or Fate;
'Tis not his face; I've sence enough to see,
That is not good, though doated on by me;
Not is't his Tongue, that has this Conquest won;
For that at least is equall'd by my own:
His Carriage can to none obliging be,
'Tis Rude, Affected, full of Vanity:
Strangely Ill-natur'd, Peevish and Unkind,
Unconstant, False, to Jealousie inclin'd,
His Temper cou'd not have so great a Pow'r,
'Tis mutable, and changes every hour:
Those vigorous Years that Women so Adore,
Are past in him: he's twice my Age, and more;
And yet I love this false, this worthless Man
With all the Passion that a Woman can;
Doat on his Imperfections, though I spy
Nothing to Love; I Love, and know not why.
Since 'tis Decreed in the dark Book of Fate
That I shou'd Love, and he shou'd be ingrate.


*'Ephelia' (fl. c.1678-82)*

18

# WHY DO I LOVE YOU, SIR?

'Why do I love' You, Sir?
Because—
The Wind does not require the Grass
To answer—Wherefore when He pass
She cannot keep Her place.

Because He knows—and
Do not You—
And We know not—
Enough for Us
The Wisdom it be so—

The Lightning—never asked an Eye
Wherefore it struck—when He was by
Because He knows it cannot speak—
And reasons not contained—
—Of Talk—
There be preferred by Daintier Folk—

The Sunrise—Sir—compelleth Me—
Because He's Sunrise—and I see—
Therefore—Then—
I love Thee—

*Emily Dickinson (1830-86)*

# VARIATIONS ON THE WORD LOVE

This is a word we use to plug
holes with. It's the right size for those warm
blanks in speech, for those red heart-
shaped vacancies on the page that look nothing
like real hearts. Add lace
and you can sell
it. We insert it also in the one empty
space on the printed form
that comes with no instructions. There are whole
magazines with not much in them
but the word *love*, you can
rub it all over your body and you
can cook with it too. How do we know
it isn't what goes on at the cool
debaucheries of slugs under damp
pieces of cardboard? As for the weed-
seedlings nosing their tough snouts up
among the lettuces, they shout it.
Love! Love! sing the soldiers, raising
their glittering knives in salute.
Then there's the two
of us. This word
is far too short for us, it has only
four letters, too sparse
to fill those deep bare
vacuums between the stars
that press on us with their deafness.
It's not love we don't wish
to fall into, but that fear.

This word is not enough but it will
have to do. It's a single
vowel in this metallic
silence, a mouth that says
O again and again in wonder
and pain, a breath, a finger-
grip on a cliffside. You can
hold on or let go.

*Margaret Atwood (b.1939)*

# THE UNFORTUNATE DAMSEL

I sowed the seeds of love
To blossom all the spring,
In April, May, or else in June,
When the small birds do sing:
A gardener standing by,
I desired him to choose for me;
He picked out the lily, the violet, and pink,
But I refused all three.
The lily I refused,
Because it faded so soon;
The violet and pink I overlooked,
Resolved was to tarry till June:
In June the red roses bud,
Oh, that is a lover for me;
But I have often aimed at the red rose-bud,
And I have gained the willow-tree.
The gardener standing by,
He prayed me to have a care,
For the thorn that grew on the red rose-bush,
A venomous thorn they were:
A venomous thorn indeed,
For still I feel the smart;
And every time I did it touch,
It pricked my tender heart.
Away you fading flowers,
No more I will you touch,
That all the world may plainly see
I loved one flower too much.

*Mrs. Fleetwood Habergham (d.1703)*

## From HOW LISA LOVED THE KING

. . . She watched all day that she might see him pass
With knights and ladies; but she said, 'Alas!
Though he should see me, it were all as one
He saw a pigeon sitting on the stone
Of wall or balcony: some coloured spot
His eye just sees, his mind regardeth not.
I have no music-touch that could bring nigh
My love to his soul's hearing. I shall die,
And he will never know who Lisa was—
The trader's child, whose soaring spirit rose
As hedge-born aloe flowers that rarest years disclose . . .'

*George Eliot (1819-80)*

# ON MONSIEUR'S DEPARTURE

I grieve and dare not show my discontent;
    I love, and yet am forced to seem to hate;
I do, yet dare not say I ever meant;
    I seem stark mute, but inwardly do prate:
I am, and not: I freeze, and yet am burn'd,
Since from myself, my other self I turn'd.

My care is like my shadow in the sun,
    Follows me flying, flies when I pursue it;
Stands and lies by me, does what I have done;
    This too familiar care does make me rue it:
No means I find to rid him from my breast,
Till by the end of things it be supprest.

Some gentler passions slide into my mind,
    For I am soft and made of melting snow;
Or be more cruel, Love, and so be kind,
    Let me or float or sink, be high or low:
Or let me live with some more sweet content,
Or die, and so forget what love e'er meant.


*Elizabeth I (1533-1603)*

24

## From A PRAYER FOR INDIFFERENCE

I ask no kind return in love,
    No tempting charm to please;
Far from the heart those gifts remove,
    That sighs for peace and ease;

Nor peace, nor ease, the heart can know,
    That, like the needle true,
Turns at the touch of joy or woe,
    But, turning, trembles too.

Far as distress the soul can wound,
    'Tis pain in each degree:
'Tis bliss but to a certain bound,
    Beyond is agony.


*Frances Greville (c.1724-89)*

# AULD ROBIN GRAY

When the sheep are in the fauld, and the kye at hame,
And a' the warld to rest are gane,
The waes o' my heart fa' in showers frae my e'e,
While my gudeman lies sound by me.

Young Jamie lo'ed me weel, and sought me for his bride;
And saving a croun he had naething else beside:
To make the croun a pund, young Jamie gaed to sea;
And the croun and the pund were baith for me.

He hadna been awa' a week but only twa,
When my father brak his arm, and the cow was stown awa';
My mother she fell sick,—and my Jamie at the sea—
And auld Robin Gray came a-courtin' me.

My father couldna work, and my mother couldna spin;
I toil'd day and night, but their bread I couldna win;
Auld Rob maintain'd them baith, and wi' tears in his e'e
Said, 'Jennie, for their sakes, O, marry me!'

My heart it said nay; I look'd for Jamie back;
But the wind it blew high, and the ship it was a wrack;
His ship it was a wrack—Why didna Jamie dee?
Or why do I live to cry, Wae's me?

My father urged me sair: my mother didna speak;
But she look'd in my face till my heart was like to break:
They gie'd him my hand, tho' my heart was in the sea;
Sae auld Robin Gray he was gudeman to me.

I hadna been a wife a week but only four,
When mournfu' as I sat on the stane at the door,
I saw my Jamie's wraith,—for I couldna think it he,
Till he said, 'I'm come hame to marry thee.'

O sair, sair did we greet, and muckle did we say;
We took but ae kiss, and I bad him gang away:
I wish that I were dead, but I'm no like to dee;
And why was I born to say, Wae's me!

I gang like a ghaist, and I carena to spin;
I daurna think on Jamie, for that wad be a sin;
But I'll do my best a gude wife aye to be,
For auld Robin Gray he is kind unto me.

*Anne Lindsay (1750-1825)*

# THE WISH

Would but indulgent Fortune send
To me a kind, and faithful Friend,
One who to Virtue's Laws is true,
And does her nicest Rules pursue;
One Pious, Lib'ral, Just and Brave,
And to his Passions not a Slave;
Who full of Honour, void of Pride,
Will freely praise, and freely chide;
But not indulge the smallest Fault,
Nor entertain one slighting Thought:
Who still the same will ever prove,
Will still instruct and still will love:
In whom I safely may confide,
And with him all my Cares divide:
Who has a large capacious Mind,
Join'd with a Knowledge unconfin'd:
A Reason bright, a Judgement true,
A Wit both quick, and solid too:
Who can of all things talk with Ease,
And whose Converse will ever please:
Who charm'd with Wit, and inward Graces,
Despises Fools with tempting Faces;
And still a beauteous Mind does prize
Above the most enchanting Eyes:
I would not envy Queens their State,
Nor once desire a happier Fate.

*Mary Chudleigh (1656-1710)*

## TO MY DEAR AND LOVING HUSBAND

If ever two were one, then surely we.
If ever man were lov'd by wife, then thee.
If ever wife was happy in a man,
Compare with me, ye woman, if you can.
I prize thy love more than whole mines of gold,
Or all the riches that the east doth hold.
My love is such that rivers cannot quench,
Nor ought but love from thee give recompence.
Thy love is such I can no way repay;
The heavens reward thee manifold I pray.
Then while we live, in love let's so perséver,
That when we love no more, we may live ever.

*Anne Bradstreet (?1613-72)*

## LINES,

*Written on Seeing My Husband's Picture,*
*painted when he was young*


Those are the features, those the smiles,
    That first engag'd my virgin heart:
I feel the pencil'd image true,
    I feel the mimic pow'r of art.

For ever on my soul engrav'd
    His glowing cheek, his manly mien;
I need not thee, thou painted shade,
    To tell me what my Love has been.

O dearer now, tho' bent with age,
    Than in the pride of blooming youth!
I knew not then his constant heart,
    I knew not then his matchless truth.

Full many a year, at random tost,
    The sport of many an adverse gale,
Together, hand in hand, we've stray'd
    O'er dreary hill, and lonely vale.

Hope only flattered to betray,
    Her keenest shafts misfortune shot:
In spite of prudence, spite of care,
    *Dependence* was our bitter lot.

Ill can'st thou bear the sneer of wealth,
    Averted looks, and rustic scorn;
For thou wert born to better hopes,
    And brighter rose thy vernal morn.

Thy ev'ning hours to want expos'd,
    I cannot, cannot bear to see:
Were but thy honest heart at ease,
    I care not what becomes of me.

But tho', my Love, the winds of woe
    Beat cold upon thy silver hairs,
Thy ANNA'S bosom still is warm;
    Affection still shall soothe thy cares.

And Conscience, with unclouded ray,
    The cottage of our age will cheer;
Friendship will lift our humble latch,
    And Pity pour her healing tear.


*Anna Sawyer (fl.1794–1801)*

# THE SLIGHTED LADY

There was a man who won a beautiful woman.
Not only was she lovely, and shaped like a woman,
But she had a beautiful mind.
She understood everything the man said to her,
She listened and smiled,
And the man possessed her and grew in ecstasy,
And he talked while the woman listened and smiled.

But there came a day when the woman understood even
     more than the man had said;
Then *she* spoke, and the man, sated with possession, and
     weary with words, slept.
He slept on the threshold of his house.
The woman was within, in a small room.

Then to the window of her room
Came a young lover with his lute,
And thus he sang:

"O, beautiful woman, who can perfect my dreams,
Take my soul into your hands
Like a clear crystal ball.
Warm it to softness at your breast,
And shape it as you will.
We two shall sing together living songs,
And walk our Paradise in an eternal noon—
Come, my Desire, I wait."

But the woman, remembering the sleeper and her faith,
Shook her good head to keep the longing from her eyes,
At which the lover sang again, and with such lusty rapture
That the sleeper waked,
And listening to the song, he said:
"My woman has bewitched this man—
He is seduced.
What folly does he sing?
This woman is no goddess, but my wife;
And no perfection, but the keeper of my house."

Whereat the woman said within her heart;
"My husband has not looked at me for many days—
He has forgot that flesh is warm,
And that the spirit hungers.
I have waited long within the house;
I freeze with dumbness, and I go."

Then she stept down from her high window
And walked with her young lover, singing to his lute.


*Anna Wickham (1884-1947)*

# AN ANSWER TO A LOVE-LETTER

Is it to me, this sad lamenting strain?
Are heaven's choicest gifts bestow'd in vain?
A plenteous fortune, and a beauteous bride,
Your love rewarded, gratify'd your pride:
Yet leaving her—'tis me that you pursue
Without one single charm, but being new.
How vile is man! how I detest their ways
Of artful falsehood, and designing praise!
Tasteless, an easy happiness you slight,
Ruin your joy, and mischief your delight.
Why should poor pug (the mimic of your kind)
Wear a rough chain, and be to box confin'd?
Some cup, perhaps, he breaks, or tears a fan,—
While roves unpunish'd the destroyer, man.
Not bound by vows, and unrestrain'd by shame,
In sport you break the heart, and rend the fame.
Not that your art can be successful here,
Th'already plunder'd need no robber-fear:
Nor sighs, nor charms, nor flatteries can move,
Too well secur'd against a second love.
Once, and but once, that devil charm'd my mind;
To reason deaf, to observation blind;
I idly hop'd (what cannot love persuade!)
My fondness equal'd, and my love repay'd;
Slow to distrust, and willing to believe,
Long hush'd my doubts, and did myself deceive:
But oh! too soon—this tale would ever last;
Sleep, sleep my wrongs, and let me think 'em past.
For you who mourn with counterfeited grief,
And ask so boldly like a begging thief,
May soon some other nymph inflict the pain,
You know so well with cruel art to feign.
Tho' long you sported have with Cupid's dart,
You may see eyes, and you may feel a heart.

So the brisk wits, who stop the evening coach,
Laugh at the fear which follows their approach;
With idle mirth, and haughty scorn despise
The passenger's pale cheek, and staring eyes:
But seiz'd by Justice, find a fright no jest,
And all the terror doubled in their breast.

*Lady Mary Wortley Montagu (1689–1762)*

## SOCIAL NOTE

Lady, lady, should you meet
One whose ways are all discreet,
One who murmurs that his wife
Is the lodestar of his life,
One who keeps assuring you
That he never was untrue,
Never loved another one . . .
Lady, lady, better run!

*Dorothy Parker (1893–1967)*

# TO J.G. ON THE NEWS OF HIS MARRIAGE

My Love? alas! I must not call you Mine,
But to your envy'd Bride that Name resign:
I must forget your lovely melting Charms,
And be fore ever Banisht from your Arms:
For ever? oh! the Horror of that Sound!
It gives my bleeding Heart a deadly wound:
While I might hope, although my Hope was vain,
It gave some Ease to my unpitty'd Pain,
But now your *Hymen*\* doth all Hope exclude,     \*marriage
And but to think is Sin; yet you intrude
On every Thought; if I but close my Eyes,
Methinks your pleasing Form besides me lies;
With every Sigh I gently breath your Name,
Yet no ill Thoughts pollute my hallow'd Flame;
'Tis pure and harmless, as a Lambent Fire,
And never mingled with a warm Desire:
All I have now to ask of Bounteous Heaven,
Is, that your Perjuries may be forgiven:
That she who you have with your Nuptials blest,
As She's the Happiest Wife, may prove the Best:
That all our Joys may light on you alone,
Then I can be contented to have none:
And never wish that you shou'd kinder be,
Than now and then, to cast a Thought on Me:
And, Madam, though the Conquest you have won,
Over my Strephon, has my hopes undone;
I'le daily beg of Heaven, he may be
Kinder to You, than he has been to Me.

'Ephelia' (fl.c.1678-82)

# SONG

Strephon hath Fashion, Wit and Youth,
    With all things else that please;
He nothing wants but Love and Truth
    To ruin me with ease:
But he is flint, and bears the Art
    To kindle fierce desire;
His pow'r inflames another's heart,
    Yet he ne'er feels the fire.

O! how it does my Soul perplex,
    When I his charms recall,
To think he shou'd despise our Sex;
    Or, what's worse, love 'em all!
My wearied Heart, like *Noah's* Dove,
    In vain has sought for rest;
Finding no hope to fix my Love,
    Returns into my Breast.

*Elizabeth Taylor (fl.c.1685–1720)*

## TO ALEXIS IN ANSWER TO HIS POEM
## AGAINST FRUITION

Since man with that inconstancy was born,
To love the absent, and the present scorn
    Why do we deck, why do we dress
    For such short-lived happiness?
    Why do we put attraction on,
Since either way 'tis we must be undone?

    They fly if honour take our part,
    Our virtue drives 'em o'er the field.
    We love 'em by too much desert,
    And oh! they fly us if we yield.
Ye gods! is there no charm in all the fair
To fix this wild, this faithless wanderer?

*Aphra Behn (1640-89)*

# TO A LADY MAKING LOVE

Good madam, when ladies are willing,
    A man must needs look like a fool;
For me I would not give a shilling
    For one who would love out of rule.

You should leave us to guess by your blushing,
    And not speak the matter so plain;
'Tis our's to write and be pushing,
    'Tis yours to affect disdain.

That you're in a terrible taking,
    By all these sweet oglings I see,
But the fruit that can fall without shaking,
    Indeed is too mellow for me.

*Lady Mary Wortley Montagu (1689-1762)*

# From THE ART OF COQUETRY

First form your artful looks with studious care,
From mild to grave, from tender to severe.
Oft on the careless youth your glances dart,
A tender meaning let each glance impart.
Whene'er he meet your looks, with modest pride
And soft confusion turn your eyes aside,
Let a soft sigh steal out, as if by chance,
Then cautious turn, and steal another glance.
Caught by these arts, with pride and hope elate,
The destined victim rushes on his fate:
Pleased, his imagined victory pursues,
And the kind maid with soft attention views,
Contemplates now her shape, her air, her face,
And thinks each feature wears an added grace;
Till gratitude, which first his bosom proves,
By slow degrees sublimed, at length he loves.
'Tis harder still to fix than gain a heart;
What's won by beauty must be kept by art.
Too kind a treatment the blest lover cloys,
And oft despair the growing flame destroys:
Sometimes with smiles receive him, sometimes tears,
And wisely balance both his hopes and fears.
Perhaps he mourns his ill-requited pains,
Condemns your sway, and strives to break his chains;
Behaves as if he now your scorn defied,
And thinks at least he shall alarm your pride:
But with indifference view the seeming change,
And let your eyes to seek new conquests range;
While his torn breast with jealous fury burns,
He hopes, despairs, adores and hates by turns;
With anguish now repents the weak deceit,
And powerful passion bears him to your feet.

*Charlotte Lennox (?1729-1804)*

## WOMEN ARE DIFFERENT . . .

You dare not let your eyes meet theirs
for more than fifteen seconds.
Cos if you do,
You know what *they're* like
Liable to cross right over
to your side of the road,
and talk 'bout
"Daughter" and
"Sister" and
all that incestuous crap
You *don't* want to hear.
No,
You dare not let your eyes meet theirs.

However,
That's not to say that
*Your* gaze can't slide over
small, tight bums
And,
Thighs carved so strong and want to
weep,
Or,
That real rude and stylish swagger,
Or hands that make you wonder
how they'd feel on *those* parts of your body.
Um hum!

It's just that,
You got to make sure that
they don't catch you out
When it's your turn to look,
Cos,
Then. . .
They'd *know.*

*Marsha Prescod*

# ONCE WE PLAYED

Once we played at love together—
    Played it smartly, if you please;
Lightly, as a windblown feather,
    Did we stake a heart apiece.

Oh, it was delicious fooling!
    In the hottest of the game,
Without thought of future cooling,
    All too quickly burned Life's flame.

In this give-and-take of glances,
    Kisses sweet as honey dews,
When we played with equal chances,
    Did you win, or did I lose?

*Mathilde Blind (1841-96)*

# GIVING

You think I give myself to you?
    Not so, my friend, you do not see
My single purpose and intent—
    To make you give myself to me.

*Nora B. Cunningham (late 19th / early 20th century)*

# RENOUNCEMENT

I must not think of thee; and, tired yet strong,
   I shun the love that lurks in all delight—
   The love of thee—and in the blue heaven's height,
And in the dearest passage of a song.
O just beyond the fairest thoughts that throng
   This breast, the thought of thee waits, hidden yet bright;
   But it must never, never come in sight;
I must stop short of thee the whole day long.

But when sleep comes to close each difficult day,
   When night gives pause to the long watch I keep,
   And all my bonds I needs must loose apart,
Must doff my will as raiment laid away,—
   With the first dream that comes with the first sleep
   I run, I run, I am gathered to thy heart.

*Alice Meynell (1847-1922)*

## AT 3 A.M.

the room contains no sound
except the ticking of the clock
which has begun to panic
like an insect, trapped
in an enormous box.

Books lie open on the carpet.

Somewhere else
you're sleeping
and beside you there's a woman
who is crying quietly
so you won't wake.

*Wendy Cope (b.1945)*

# SONNET FROM THE PORTUGUESE VI

Go from me.  Yet I feel that I shall stand
Henceforward in thy shadow. Nevermore
Alone upon the threshold of my door
Of individual life, I shall command
The uses of my soul, nor lift my hand
Serenely in the sunshine as before,
Without the sense of that which I forbore, . .
Thy touch upon the palm. The widest land
Doom takes to part us, leaves thy heart in mine
With pulses that beat double. What I do
And what I dream include thee, as the wine
Must taste of its own grapes. And when I sue
God for myself, He hears that name of thine,
And sees within my eyes, the tears of two.

*Elizabeth Barrett Browning (1806-61)*

# SONNET

I still shall smile and go my careless way;
Dawn shall not see my tears,—nor shall night hear
Through broken murmurings thy name sound clear,
Nor catch old dreams of love that drift and sway—
The wistful ghosts of a forgotten day.
Nor shall the lilt of Spring, nor Autumns sere,
Awake my heart to pain, to pulsing fear,
Nor lure me from my days serene and grey.

Only one place my steps may never go,
One moorland path my feet may never climb.
O heart of mine!—the heather springy—sweet,
The loch a silver shimmer far below—
Forget that day, the haunting scent of thyme;
Forget the love all shattered at my feet.

*Maimie A. Richardson (fl.1920s)*

# THE LETTER

I take my pen in hand
>*there was a meadow*
*Beside a field of oats, beside a wood,*
*Beside a road, beside a day spread out*
*Green at the edges, yellow at the heart.*
*The dust lifted a little, a finger's breadth,*
*The word of the wood pigeon travelled slow,*
*A slow half pace behind the tick of time.*

To tell you I am well, and thinking of you
*And of the walk through the meadow, and of another walk*
*Along the neat piled ruin of the town*
*Under a pale heaven, empty of all but death*
*And rain beginning. The river ran beside.*

It has been a long time since I wrote. I have no news.
*I put my head between my hands and hope*
*My heart will choke me. I put out my hand*
*To touch you and touch air. I turn to sleep*
*And find a nightmare, hollowness and fear.*

And by the way, I have had no letter now
For eight weeks, it must be
>*a long eight weeks,*
*Because you have nothing to say, nothing at all,*
*Not even to record your emptiness*
*Or guess what's to become of you without love.*

I know that you have cares,
*Ashes to shovel, broken glass to mend*
*And many a cloth to patch before the sunset.*

Write to me soon, and tell me how you are.
*If you still tremble, sweat and glower, still stretch*
*A hand for me at dusk, play me the tune,*
*Show me the leaves and towers, the lamb, the rose.*

Because I always wish to hear of you
*And feel my heart swell, and the blood run out*
*At the ungraceful syllable of your name*
*Said through the scent of stocks, the little snore of fire,*
*The shoreless waves of symphony, the murmuring night.*

I will end this letter now. I am yours with love.
*Always with love, with love.*


*Elizabeth Riddell (b.1910)*

# CARREFOUR

O you,
Who came upon me once
Stretched under apple-trees just after bathing,
Why did you not strangle me before speaking
Rather than fill me with the wild white honey of your words
And then leave me to the mercy
Of the forest bees?

*Amy Lowell (1874-1925)*

# THE VAIN ADVICE

Ah, gaze not on those eyes! forbear
That soft enchanting voice to hear:
Not looks of basilisks give surer death,
Nor *Syrens* sing with more destructive breath.

Fly, if thy freedom thou'dst maintain,
Alas! I feel th'advice is vain!
A heart, whose safety but in flight does lie,
Is too far lost to have the power to fly.

*Catherine Cockburn (1679-1749)*

# SIENA

*"L'anima non avra giammai l'oblio, giammai l'oblio, giammai . . ."*

Whilst thou art far away, I am at peace,
As some poor wretch, delivered from the rack,
Enjoys the slumber of a doubtful ease
Knowing he must be haled to torture back.

In this embattled city of old days,
The flower of beauty born of blood and fire,
My footsteps wander through the narrow ways,
And seek in vain the soul of my desire;

I feast upon my dreams' immortal food,
But when there comes again the thought of thee,
It is as if slow heavy drops of blood
Dripped from a wound within unceasingly.

*Lily Thicknesse (fl. early 20th century)*

## WHY?

Why did you come, with your enkindled eyes
And mountain-look, across my lower way,
And take the vague dishonour from my day
By luring me from paltry things, to rise
And stand beside you, waiting wistfully
The looming of a larger destiny?

Why did you with strong fingers fling aside
The gates of possibility, and say
With vital voice the words I dream to-day?
Before, I was not much unsatisfied:
But since a god has touched me and departed,
I run through every temple, broken-hearted.

*Mary Webb (1881–1927)*

# THE REQUEST OF ALEXIS

Give, give me back that Trifle you despise,
Give back my Heart, with all its Injuries:
Tho' by your Cruelty it wounded be,
The Thing is yet of wond'rous Use to me.
A gen'rous Conqueror, when the Battle's won,
Bestows a Charity on the Undone:
If from the well aim'd Stroke no Hope appear,
He kills the Wretch, and shews Compassion there:
But you, Barbarian! keep alive in Pain,
A lasting Trophy of Unjust Disdain.

*Sarah Dixon (fl.1716–45)*

## LOVE ME AT LAST

Love me at last, or if you will not,
Leave me;
Hard words could never, as these half-words,
Grieve me:
Love me at last—or leave me.

Love me at last, or let the last word uttered
Be but your own;
Love me, or leave me—as a cloud, a vapor,
Or a bird flown.
Love me at last—I am but sliding water
Over a stone.


*Alice Corbin (late 19th/early 20th century)*

## REMEDIA AMORIS
*To Henry Cromwell Esq;*


*Love*, and the *Gout* invade the idle *Brain*,
Bus'ness prevents the *Passion*, and the *Pain*:
*Ceres*, and *Bacchus*, envious of our *Ease*,
Blow up the *Flame*, and heighten the *Disease*.
Withdraw the *Fewel*, and the *Fire* goes out;
*Hard Beds*, and *Fasting*, cure both *Love* and *Gout*.


*Elizabeth Thomas (1675-1731)*

# COMMENT

Oh, life is a glorious cycle of song,
A medley of extemporanea;
And love is a thing that can never go wrong;
And I am Marie of Rumania.

*Dorothy Parker (1893-1967)*

## TO MY YOUNG LOVER

Incautious *Youth*, why do'st thou so mis-place
Thy fine *Encomiums* on an o'er-blown Face;
Which after all the Varnish of thy Quill,
Its *Pristine* wrinkles shew apparent still:
Nor is it in the power of *Youth* to move
An *Age-chill'd* heart to any strokes of Love.
Then chuse some budding *Beauty*, which in time
May crown thy Wishes in thy blooming prime:
For nought can make a more preposterous show,
Than *April*'s Flowers stuck on St. *Michael*'s Bow.
To consecrate thy first-born Sighs to me,
A *superannuated* Deity;
Makes that Idolatry and deadly Sin,
Which otherwise had only *Venial* been.

*Jane Barker (1652-1727)*

## SONNET X

Oh, my beloved, have you thought of this:
How in the years to come unscrupulous Time,
More cruel than Death, will tear you from my kiss,
And make you old, and leave me in my prime?
How you and I, who scale together yet
A little while the sweet, immortal height
No pilgrim may remember or forget,
As sure as the world turns, some granite night
Shall lie awake and know the gracious flame
Gone out forever on the mutual stone;
And call to mind how on the day you came
I was a child, and you a hero grown?
And the night pass, and the strange morning break
Upon our anguish for each other's sake!

*Edna St Vincent Millay (1892-1950)*

# HEART AND MIND

Said the Lion to the Lioness—'When you are amber dust,—
No more a raging fire like the heat of the Sun
(No liking but all lust)—
Remember still the flowering of the amber blood and bone
The rippling of bright muscles like a sea,
Remember the rose-prickles of bright paws
Though we shall mate no more
Till the fire of that sun the heart and the moon-cold bone
        are one.'

Said the Skeleton lying upon the sands of Time—
'The great gold planet that is the mourning heat of the Sun
Is greater than all gold, more powerful
Than the tawny body of a Lion that fire consumes
Like all that grows or leaps . . . so is the heart
More powerful than all dust. Once I was Hercules
Or Samson, strong as the pillars of the seas:
But the flames of the heart consumed me, and the mind
Is but a foolish wind.'

Said the Sun to the Moon—'When you are but a lonely
        white crone,
And I, a dead King in my golden armour somewhere in a
        dark wood,
Remember only this of our hopeless love
That never till Time is done
Will the fire of the heart and the fire of the mind be one.'


*Edith Sitwell (1887-1964)*

# SECRET FLOWERS

Is love a light for me? A steady light,
A lamp within whose pallid pool I dream
Over old love-books? Or is it a gleam,
A lantern coming towards me from afar
Down a dark mountain? Is my love a star?
Ah me!—so high above so coldly bright!

The fire dances. Is my love a fire
Leaping down the twilight muddy and bold?
Nay, I'd be frightened of him. I'm too cold
For quick and eager loving. There's a gold
Sheen on these flower petals as they fold
More truly mine, more like to my desire.

The flower petals fold. They are by the sun
Forgotten. In a shadowy wood they grow
Where the dark trees keep up a to-and-fro
Shadowy waving. Who will watch them shine
When I have dreamed my dream? Ah, darling mine,
Find them, gather them for me one by one.


*Katherine Mansfield (1888-1923)*

## 'THE SEA'S WASH IN THE HOLLOW
## OF THE HEART. . .'
(C.W.G.)


Turn from that road's beguiling ease; return
to your hunger's turret. Enter, climb the stair
chill with disuse, where the croaking toad of time
regards from shimmering eyes your slow ascent
and the drip, drip, of darkness glimmers on stone
to show you how your longing waits alone.
What alchemy shines from under that shut door,
spinning out gold from the hollow of the heart?

Enter the turret of your love, and lie
close in the arms of the sea; let in new suns
that beat and echo in the mind like sounds
risen from sunken cities lost to fear;
let in the light that answers your desire
awakening at midnight with the fire,
until its magic burns the wavering sea
and flames caress the windows of your tower.


*Denise Levertov (b.1923)*

# UPHOLD ME

And still my feelings sprout richest
in the furrow ploughed by my father:
caress me as a daughter
to gather a total harvest.
I accept you with every blemish,
as I did the man in my childhood,
as a measure of my own value;
be David to make me Bathsheba,
elaborate me with legends,
uphold me in the image
I formed of myself when I was
indomitable like grass
and passion lay fallow.

*Karen Gershon (b.1923)*

## OF EARTHLY LOVE

For I have read
in the long poems written long ago by men and women
    writing of their love
that time might go
like a breath blowing in the night
and they be dead
but still their love would beacon like Warwick light.

It is not so.

The illumination's done
that lit the fondest ship its phantom way,
the lighthouse has been ruined and the rock on
    which it stood has crumbled quite away,
the flesh that once was warm at last has kept—
    hidden from the eye of the impartial sun—
its bodily faith, and here to-night has slept
where love, all love, is done.

Insatiate longing, let it be enough
to have been briefly of immortal stuff.


*Susanna Valentine Mitchell (fl.1920s)*

# TOUCH WOOD

Touch wood, be humble, never dare to say
That this is joy lest satisfaction throw
A shade on love which now (while roots still grow)
Stands like the proudest chestnut tree in May
With all its candles burning. Passions sway:
This has no tide nor any ebb and flow;
It has no evening, no red afterglow,
And needs no moon to keep the night at bay.

But since most lovers falter or contend,
And all their promises and all their powers
Drift towards a common grave, what chance have we?
Poets keep the past and priests eternity;
Only the day, the flying day is ours,
But while we hold it fast it cannot end.

*Helen Foley (1896-1937)*

# I WOULD LIVE IN YOUR LOVE

I would live in your love as the sea-grasses live in the sea,
Borne up by each wave as it passes, drawn down by each wave
    that recedes;
I would empty my soul of the dreams that have gathered
    in me,
I would beat with your heart as it beats, I would follow your
    soul as it leads.

*Sara Teasdale (1884-1933)*

# I REMEMBER

By the first of August
the invisible beetles began
to snore and the grass was
as tough as hemp and was
no colour—no more than
the sand was a colour and
we had worn our bare feet
bare since the twentieth
of June and there were times
we forgot to wind up your
alarm clock and some nights
we took our gin warm and neat
from old jelly glasses while
the sun blew out of sight
like a red picture hat and
one day I tied my hair back
with a ribbon and you said
that I looked almost like
a puritan lady and what
I remember best is that
the door to your room was
the door to mine.

*Anne Sexton (1928-74)*

# SONG

O Love! that stronger art than wine,
Pleasing delusion, witchery divine,
Wont to be prized above all wealth,
Disease that has more joys than health;
Though we blaspheme thee in our pain,
And of thy tyranny complain,
We are all bettered by thy reign.

What reason never can bestow
We to this useful passion owe;
Love wakes the dull from sluggish ease,
And learns a clown the art to please,
Humbles the vain, kindles the cold,
Makes misers free, and cowards bold;
'Tis he reforms the sot from drink,
And teaches airy fops to think.

When full brute appetite is fed,
And choked the glutton lies and dead,
Thou new spirits dost dispense
And 'finest the gross delights of sense:
Virtue's unconquerable aid
That against Nature can persuade,
And makes a roving mind retire
Within the bounds of just desire;
Cheerer of age, youth's kind unrest,
And half the heaven of the blest!

*Aphra Behn (1640-89)*

## A SONG

Love, thou art best of Human Joys,
  Our chiefest Happiness below;
All other Pleasures are but Toys,
Musick without Thee is but Noise,
    And Beauty but an empty show.

Heav'n, who knew best what Man wou'd move,
  And raise his Thoughts above the Brute;
Said, Let him Be, and Let him Love;
That must alone his Soul improve,
    Howe'er Philosophers dispute.


*Ann Finch (1661-1720)*

# THE QUEST

High, hollowed in green
above the rocks of reason
lies the crater lake
whose ice the dreamer breaks
to find a summer season.

'He will plunge like a plummet down
far into hungry tides'
they cry, but as the sea
climbs to a lunar magnet
so the dreamer pursues
the lake where love resides.

*Denise Levertov (b.1923)*

# THE TRUCE

There is a truce . . . O lovers, tell
The hungering world . . . you know it well;
Swords laid aside, a heavenly pause
In the assault of love's cruel wars.

Then the lover's bending head
From his smooth throat like Adam's turns,
And gentle kisses close her eyes
Like hesitating butterflies;
Unwavering the passion burns
Tranced, tranced in visions softer than
The fabled schemes of Kubla Khan.

It is for this that men make war,
Breathe gold like air, go mad, or die,
Spend years as grey as moth-wing tips,
Scale peaks, and rim the sea with ships.

All for this truce, this trance of love,
When the whole world hovers like a dove,
And gentle darkness shuts the eyes
With kisses soft as butterflies.

*Stella Gibbons (b.1902)*

# A BIRTHDAY

My heart is like a singing bird
Whose nest is in a watered shoot;
My heart is like an apple tree
Whose boughs are bent with thickset fruit;
My heart is like a rainbow shell
That paddles in a halcyon sea;
My heart is gladder than all these
Because my love is come to me.

Raise me a dais of silk and down;
Hang it with vair and purple dyes;
Carve it in doves and pomegranates,
And peacocks with a hundred eyes;
Work it in gold and silver grapes,
In leaves and silver fleurs-de-lys;
Because the birthday of my life
Is come, my love is come to me.

*Christina Rossetti (1830-94)*

# VISION

To-day there have been lovely things
I never saw before;
Sunlight through a jar of marmalade;
A blue gate;
A rainbow
In soapsuds on dishwater;
Candlelight on butter;
The crinkled smile of a little girl
Who had new shoes with tassels;
A chickadee on a thorn-apple;
Empurpled mud under a willow,
Where white geese slept;
White ruffled curtains sifting moonlight
On the scrubbed kitchen floor;
The under side of a white-oak leaf;
Ruts in the road at sunset;
An egg yolk in a blue bowl.

My love kissed my eyes last night.

*May Thielgaard Watts (fl.1920s)*

## LOVE LETTER

Not easy to state the change you made.
If I'm alive now, then I was dead,
Though, like a stone, unbothered by it,
Staying put according to habit.
You didn't just toe me an inch, no—
Nor leave me to set my small bald eye
Skyward again, without hope, of course,
Of apprehending blueness, or stars.

That wasn't it. I slept, say: a snake
Masked among black rocks as a black rock
In the white hiatus of winter—
Like my neighbors, taking no pleasure
In the million perfectly-chiseled
Cheeks alighting each moment to melt
My cheek of basalt. They turned to tears,
Angels weeping over dull natures,
But didn't convince me. Those tears froze.
Each dead head had a visor of ice.

And I slept on like a bent finger.
The first thing I saw was sheer air
And the locked drops rising in a dew
Limpid as spirits. Many stones lay
Dense and expressionless round about.
I didn't know what to make of it.
I shone, mica-scaled, and unfolded
To pour myself out like a fluid
Among bird feet and the stems of plants.
I wasn't fooled. I knew you at once.

Tree and stone glittered, without shadows.
My finger-length grew lucent as glass.
I started to bud like a March twig:
An arm and a leg, an arm, a leg.
From stone to cloud, so I ascended.
Now I resemble a sort of god
Floating through the air in my soul-shift
Pure as a pane of ice. It's a gift.

*Sylvia Plath (1932-63)*

# PASTORAL DIALOGUE

Remember when you love, from that same hour
Your peace you put into your lover's power;
From that same hour from him you laws receive,
And as he shall ordain, you joy, or grieve,
Hope, fear, laugh, weep; Reason aloof does stand,
Disabled both to act, and to command.
Oh cruel fetters! rather wish to feel
On your soft limbs, the galling weight of steel;
Rather to bloody wounds oppose your breast.
No ill, by which the body can be pressed
You will so sensible a torment find
As shackles on your captived mind.
The mind from heaven its high descent did draw,
And brooks uneasily any other law
Than what from Reason dictated shall be.
Reason, a kind of innate deity,
Which only can adapt to ev'ry soul
A yoke so fit and light, that the control
All liberty excells; so sweet a sway,
The same 'tis to be happy, and obey;
Commands so wise, and with rewards so dressed,
That the according soul replies 'I'm blessed'.

*Anne Killigrew (1660-85)*

## From A VALENTINE

When to Love's influence woman yields,
She loves for life! and daily feels
Progressive tenderness!—each hour
Confirms, extends, the tyrant's power!
Her lover is her god! her fate!—
Vain pleasures, riches, worldly state,
Are trifles all!—each sacrifice
Becomes a dear and valued prize,
If made for him, e'en tho' he proves
Forgetful of their former loves!

*Elizabeth Trefusis (fl.c.1808)*

## CUPID LOST

Late in the Forest I did Cupid See
    Colde, wet, and crying he had lost his way,
    And being blind was farther like to stray:
    Which sight a kind compassion bred in me,

I kindly took, and dried him, while that he
    Poor child complain'd he starved was with stay,
    And pined for want of his accustom'd play,
    For none in that wild place his host would be,

I glad was of his finding, thinking sure
    This service should my freedom still procure,
    And in my arms I took him then unharmed,

Carrying him safe unto a myrtle bower
    But in the way he made me feel his power,
    Burning my heart who had him kindly warmed.


*Mary Wroth (?1586-?1640)*

# TO CUPID

Child, with many a childish wile,
Timid look, and blushing smile,
Downy wings to steal thy way,
Gilded bow, and quiver gay,
Who in thy simple mien would trace
The tyrant of the human race?

Who is he whose flinty heart
Hath not felt the flying dart?
Who is he that from the wound
Hath not pain and pleasure found?
Who is he that hath not shed
Curse and blessing on thy head?

*Joanna Baillie (1762-1851)*

# SONG

Love, a child, is ever crying;
Please him, and he straight is flying;
Give him, he the more is craving,
Never satisfied with having.

His desires have no measure;
Endless folly is his treasure;
What he promiseth he breaketh;
Trust not one word that he speaketh.

He vows nothing but false matter;
And to cozen you will flatter;
Let him gain the hand, he'll leave you,
And still glory to deceive you.

He will triumph in your wailing;
And yet cause be of your failing:
These his virtues are, and slighter
Are his gifts, his favours lighter.

Fathers are as firm in staying;
Wolves no fiercer in their preying:
As a child then, leave him crying;
Nor seek him so given to flying.

*Mary Wroth (?1586-?1640)*

## From ASPECTS OF LOVE

Love? We should smother it
And push it up the chimney—
He said, half meaning it.
We know now what he intended
For finding love at their door
On a cold night, people—if they are wise—
Will push it up the chimney into the smoke before
It wails at them with such clenched desire
As will bring into the quiet house
The significant ecstatic loss.

*Ruth Miller (1919-69)*

# THE FARMER'S BRIDE

Three Summers since I chose a maid,
Too young maybe—but more's to do
At harvest-time than bide and woo.
When us was wed she turned afraid
Of love and me and all things human;
Like the shut of a winter's day
Her smile went out, and 'twadn't a woman—
More like a little frightened fay.
One night, in the Fall, she runned away.

"Out 'mong the sheep, her be," they said,
Should properly have been abed;
But sure enough she wadn't there
Lying awake with her wide brown stare.
So over seven-acre field and up-along across the down
We chased her, flying like a hare
Before our lanterns. To Church-Town
All in a shiver and a scare
We caught her, fetched her home at last
And turned the key upon her, fast.

She does the work about the house
As well as most, but like a mouse:
Happy enough to cheat and play
With birds and rabbits and such as they,
So long as men-folk keep away
"Not near, not near!" her eyes beseech
When one of us comes within reach.
The women say that beasts in stall
Look round like children at her call.
I've hardly heard her speak at all.
Shy as a leveret, swift as he,
Straight and slight as a young larch tree,
Sweet as the first wild violets, she,
To her wild self. But what to me?

The short days shorten and the oaks are brown,
The blue smoke rises to the low grey sky,
One leaf in the still air falls slowly down,
A magpie's spotted feathers lie
On the black earth spread white with rime,
The berries redden up to Christmas-time.
What's Christmas-time without there be
Some other in the house than we!

She sleeps up in the attic there
Alone, poor maid. 'Tis but a stair
Betwixt us. Oh! my God! the down,
The soft young down of her, the brown,
The brown of her—her eyes, her hair, her hair!

*Charlotte Mew (1869-1928)*

# MARRIAGE

No more alone sleeping, no more alone waking,
    Thy dreams divided, thy prayers in twain;
Thy merry sisters tonight forsaking,
    Never shall we see, maiden, again.

Never shall we see thee, thine eyes glancing.
    Flashing with laughter and wild in glee,
Under the mistletoe kissing and dancing,
    Wantonly free.

There shall come a matron walking sedately,
    Low-voiced, gentle, wise in reply.
Tell me, O tell me, can I love her greatly?
    All for her sake must the maiden die!

*Mary Coleridge (1861-1907)*

## TWO TRUTHS

'Darling,' he said, 'I never meant
    To hurt you;' and his eyes were wet.
'I would not hurt you for the world:
    Am I to blame if I forget?'

'Forgive my selfish tears!' she cried,
    'Forgive! I knew that it was not
Because you meant to hurt me, sweet—
    I knew it was that you forgot!'

But all the same, deep in her heart
    Rankled this thought, and rankles yet,—
'When love is at its best, one loves
    So much that he cannot forget.'

*Helen Hunt Jackson (1830-85)*

# From LETTER TO MISS E.B. ON MARRIAGE

Mankind should hope, in wedlock's state,
A friend to find as well as mate:
And ere the charm of person fails,
Enquire what merit there remains,
That may, by help of their wise pate,
Be taught through life to bless the state;
And oft they'd find, by their own fire,
What they in others so admire.
But as 'tis law that each good wife
Should true submission show for life,
What's right at home they often slight,
What's right abroad shines very bright.

Each female would have regal power,
But every male wants something more;
And that same balsam to the mind,
Which both would in compliance find,
Is, to this very time and hour,
Miscalled by them the want of power.
Then right of privilege they claim,
For every fair to vow a flame,
Which we are bound, with partial eye,
To find of true platonic dye;
For they've so fixed the certain rule,
How far with ladies they may fool,
That 'tis impossible they can
Go wrong—though not a man
Among them all would patience find,
If lady-wife should be inclined
To praise each swain, whose face or wit
Might chance her sprightly mind to hit.

Then there's something in the mind,
That is not only just—but kind;
That's fixed to neither taste nor sense,
Nor to be taught by eloquence;
But yet is that which gives a grace
To every feature of the face;
And is the surest chance for ease:
I mean a strong desire to please.
But own I must (though 'tis with shame)
Both parties are in this to blame;
They take great pains to come together,
Then squabble for a straw or feather;
And oft I fear a spark of pride
Prevails too much on either side.

Then hear, my girl—if 'tis your lot
To marry, be not this forgot:
That neither sex must think to find
Perfection in the human kind;
Each has a fool's cap—and a bell—
And, what is worse, can't always tell
(While they have got it on their head)
How far astray they may be led.
Let it be then your mutual care,
That never both at once may wear
This fatal mark of reason's loss,
That whirlwind-like the soul does toss.
Obtain this point, and friendship's
power
Will rise and bless each future hour.

*Mary Savage (fl.1763-77)*

# ON THE DEATH OF MRS. BOWES

Hail, happy bride, for thou art truly blest!
Three months of rapture, crown'd with endless rest.
Merit like yours was Heav'n's peculiar care,
You lov'd yet tasted happiness sincere.
To you the sweets of love were only shown,
The sure succeeding bitter dregs unknown;
You had not yet the fatal change deplor'd,
The tender lover for th' imperious lord:
Nor felt the pain that jealous fondness brings:
Nor felt, that coldness from possession springs.
Above your sex, distinguish'd in your fate,
You trusted yet experienc'd no deceit;
Soft were your hours, and wing'd with pleasure flew;
No vain repentance gave a sigh to you:
And if superior bliss Heaven can bestow,
With fellow-angels you enjoy it now.

*Lady Mary Wortley Montagu (1689-1762)*

# THE HONEYMOON IS OVER

The honeymoon is over
And he has left for work
Whistling something obvious from La Bohème
And carrying a brown calfskin attaché case
I never dreamed he was capable of owning,
Having started the day
With ten pushups and a cold shower
Followed by a hearty breakfast.

(What do we actually have in common?)

The honeymoon is over
And I am dry-mopping the floor
In a green Dacron dry-mopping outfit from Saks,
Wondering why I'm not dancing in the dark,
Or rejecting princes,
Or hearing people gasp at my one-man show,
My god, so beautiful and so gifted!

(The trouble is I never knew a prince.)

The honeymoon is over
And we find that dining by candlelight makes us squint,
And that all the time
I was letting him borrow my comb and hang up his wet
    raincoat in my closet
I was really waiting
To stop letting him.
And that all the time
He was saying how he loved my chicken pot pie,
He was really waiting
To stop eating it.

(I guess they call this getting to know each other.)

*Judith Viorst*

# THE FAITHFUL WIFE

I am away from home
A hundred miles from the blue curtains
I made at Christmas and the table
My grandfather brought back from Sorrento.
I am a career woman at a conference.
I love my husband. I value
Both what I own and what I do.

I left the forsythias half yellow,
The bluebells—lifted from a wood in Suffolk
Last year—still tight, the mint surfacing.
I must sweep the paths when I get back.

And here for the past week you and I
Have been conducting a non-affair
That could not even be called flirtation
That could not be called anything
Except unusually straightforward desire,
Adultery in the heart.
Life is so short.

The programme is ending.
11.30—Conference disperses.
I watch everybody leaving.
It feels like grief, like the guillotine.

Your turn now; go home
With the 'Good-bye, love'
You use to every personable woman.
Get in your large car which ten years ago
Was full of sand and children's things
On summer evenings.
You are middle-aged now, as I am.
Write your notes up,
Fix the rattling window,
Keep your marriage vows. As I shall.

*Patricia Beer (b.1924)*

## ON LOVING ONCE
## AND LOVING OFTEN

Once loving is a gen'ral Fashion,
   To Nature 'tis a Tribute paid:
But, loving often shews that Passion
   Despises Reason's feeble Aid.

*Elizabeth Tollet (1694-1754)*

# THE FORSAKEN WIFE

Methinks, 'tis strange you can't afford
One *pitying Look*, one *parting Word*;
HUMANITY claims this as due,
But what's HUMANITY to you?

    *Cruel Man!* I am not *Blind*,
Your *Infidelity* I find;
Your want of *Love*, my *Ruin* shows,
My broken *Heart*, your broken *Vows*.
Yet maugre* all your rigid *Hate*,        *in spite of
I will be TRUE in spite of *Fate*;
And one *Preheminence* I'll claim,
To be for ever *still the same*.

    Show me a *Man* that dare be TRUE,
That dares to *suffer* what I do;
That can for *ever Sigh* unheard,
And ever *Love* without Regard:
I then will own your *Prior* Claim
To LOVE, to HONOUR, and to FAME:
But 'till that time, my *Dear*, adieu,
I yet SUPERIOR am to you.

*Elizabeth Thomas (1675-1731)*

## I MADE A HOUSE
## OF HOUSELESSNESS

I made a house of houselessness,
A garden of your going:
And seven trees of seven wounds
You gave me, all unknowing:
I made a feast of golden grief
That you so lordly left me,
I made a bed of all the smiles
Whereof your lip bereft me:
I made a sun of your delay,
Your daily loss, his setting:
I made a wall of all your words
And a lock of your forgetting.


*Rose O'Neill (late 19th/early 20th century)*

## NOW I HAVE NOTHING

Now I have nothing.  Even the joy of loss
Even the dreams I had I now am losing.
Only this thing I know; that you are using
My heart as a stone to bear your foot across . . .
I am glad I am glad the stone is of your choosing . . .

*Stella Benson (1892-1933)*

# HESITATE TO CALL

Lived to see you throwing
Me aside. That fought
Like netted fish inside me. Saw you throbbing
In my syrups. Saw you sleep. And lived to see
That all that all flushed down
The refuse. Done?
It lives in me.
You live in me. Malignant.
Love, you ever want me, don't.

*Louise Glück (b.1943)*

## NO, GO ON

For years he's gone over her parting words,
the ones she couldn't pack. They are printed

in the circles under his eyes. They come to mind
each night at 5 a.m., when the first trains start

and the moon bottles itself outside his door.
He is caught like a wheel on her shimmering track.

Over breakfast the rush hour begins and he wants
me to wait, starting another sentence that he just

lets fall away. And I'm saying: *no, go on, finish what
you were about to* ... *I'm with you. I'm following so far.*

*Maura Dooley (b.1957)*

## SONNET II

Time does not bring relief; you all have lied
Who told me time would ease me of my pain!
I miss him in the weeping of the rain;
I want him at the shrinking of the tide;
The old snows melt from every mountain-side,
And last year's leaves are smoke in every lane;
But last year's bitter loving must remain
Heaped on my heart, and my old thoughts abide!
There are a hundred places where I fear
To go, so with his memory they brim!
And entering with relief some quiet place
Where never fell his foot or shone his face
I say, "There is no memory of him here!"
And so stand stricken, so remembering him!

*Edna St. Vincent Millay (1892-1950)*

# FIRST FAREWELL TO J.G.

Farewell my dearer half, joy of my heart,
Heaven only knows how loth I am to part:
Whole Months but hours seem, when you are here,
When absent, every Minute is a Year:
Might I but always see thy charming Face,
I'de live on Racks, and wish no easier place.
But we must part, your Interest says we must;
Fate, me no longer with such Treasure trust.
I wou'd not tax you with Inconstancy,
Yet *Strephon*, you are not so kind as I:
No Interest, no nor Fate it self has pow'r
To tempt me from the Idol I adore:
But since you needs will go, may *Africk* be
Kinder to you, than *Europe* is to me:
May all you meet and every thing you view
Give you such Transport as I met in you.
May no sad thoughts disturb your quiet mind,
Except you'l think of her you left behind.

*'Ephelia'* (*fl.c.*1678-82)

# THE GIFT

What can I give you, my lord, my lover,
You who have given the world to me,
Showed me the light and the joy that cover
The wild sweet earth and the restless sea?

All that I have are gifts of your giving—
If I gave them again, you would find them old,
And your soul would weary of always living
Before the mirror my life would hold.

What shall I give you, my lord, my lover?
The gift that breaks the heart in me:
I bid you awake at dawn and discover
I have gone my way and left you free.

*Sara Teasdale (1884-1933)*

# A MOMENT

The clouds had made a crimson crown
    Above the mountains high.
The stormy sun was going down
    In a stormy sky.

Why did you let your eyes so rest on me,
    And hold your breath between?
In all the ages this can never be
    As if it had not been.

*Mary Elizabeth Coleridge (1861-1907)*

# THE LOOK

Strephon kissed me in the spring,
  Robin in the fall,
But Colin only looked at me
  And never kissed at all.

Strephon's kiss was lost in jest,
  Robin's lost in play,
But the kiss in Colin's eyes
  Haunts me night and day.

*Sara Teasdale (1884-1933)*

## TO LYSANDER

*(On some verses he writ, and asking more for his heart
than it was worth.)*


Take back the heart you with such caution give,
    Take the fond valu'd trifle back:
I hate love merchants that a trade wou'd drive
    And meanly cunning bargains make.

I care not how the busy market goes
    And scorn to chaffer for a price:
Love does one staple rate on all impose,
    Nor leaves it to the trader's choice.

A heart requires a heart unfeign'd and true,
    Though subtly you advance the price;
And ask a rate that simple love ne'er knew
    And the free trade monopolize.

An humble slave the buyer must become,
    She must not bate a look or glance
You will have all or you'll have none;
    See how love's market you inhance.

It's not enough I gave you heart for heart,
    But I must add my lips and eyes;
I must no smile or friendly kiss impart;
    But you must dun me with advice . . .

Be just, my lovely swain, and do not take
    Freedoms you'll not to me allow:
O give Aminta so much freedom back
    That she may rove as well as you.

Let us then love upon the honest square
    Since interest neither have design'd,
For the sly gamester, who ne'er plays me fair
    Must trick for trick expect to find.


*Aphra Behn (1640-89)*

# A SONG

Strephon, your breach of faith and trust
    Affords me no surprise;
A man who grateful was, or just,
    Might make my wonder rise.

That heart to you so fondly tied,
    With pleasure wore its chain,
But from your cold neglectful pride,
    Found liberty again.

For this no wrath inflames my mind,
    My thanks are due to thee;
Such thanks as gen'rous victors find,
    Who set their captives free.

*Laetitia Pilkington (?1712-50)*

# FREEDOM

Now heaven be thanked. I am out of love again!
I have been long a slave, and now am free:
I have been tortured, and am eased of pain:
I have been blind, and now my eyes can see:
I have been lost, and now my way lies plain:
I have been caged, and now I hold the key:
I have been mad, and now at last am sane:
I am wholly I that was but half of me.
So a free man, my dull proud path I plod,
Who, tortured, blind, mad, caged, was once a God.

*Jan Struther (1901-53)*

# COAT

Sometimes I have wanted
to throw you off
like a heavy coat.

Sometimes I have said
you would not let me
breathe or move.

But now that I am free
to choose light clothes
or none at all

I feel the cold
and all the time I think
how warm it used to be.


*Vicki Feaver (b.1943)*

# SONNET XLI

I, being born a woman and distressed
By all the needs and notions of my kind,
Am urged by your propinquity to find
Your person fair, and feel a certain zest
To bear your body's weight upon my breast:
So subtly is the fume of life designed,
To clarify the pulse and cloud the mind,
And leave me once again undone, possessed.
Think not for this, however, the poor reason
Of my stout blood against my staggering brain,
I shall remember you with love, or season
My scorn with pity let me make it plain:
I find this frenzy insufficient reason
For conversation when we meet again.

*Edna St. Vincent Millay (1892-1950)*

# AGAINST COUPLING

I write in praise of the solitary act:
of not feeling a trespassing tongue
forced into one's mouth, one's breath
smothered, nipples crushed against the
ribcage, and that metallic tingling
in the chin set off by a certain odd nerve:

unpleasure. Just to avoid those eyes would help—
such eyes as a young girl draws life from,
listening to the vegetal
rustle within her, as his gaze
stirs polypal fronds in the obscure
sea-bed of her body, and her own eyes blur.

There is much to be said for abandoning
this no longer novel exercise—
for not 'participating in
a total experience'—when
one feels like the lady in Leeds who
had seen *The Sound of Music* eighty-six times;

or more, perhaps, like the school drama mistress
producing *A Midsummer Night's Dream*
for the seventh year running, with
yet another cast from 5B.
Pyramus and Thisbe are dead, but
the hole in the wall can still be troublesome.

I advise you, then, to embrace it without
encumbrance.  No need to set the scene,
dress up (or undress), make speeches.
Five minutes of solitude are
enough—in the bath, or to fill
that gap between the Sunday papers and lunch.

*Fleur Adcock (b.1934)*

## SPINSTER

Now this particular girl
During a ceremonious april walk
With her latest suitor
Found herself, of a sudden, intolerably struck
By the bird's irregular babel
And the leaves' litter.

By this tumult afflicted, she
Observed her lover's gestures unbalance the air,
His gait stray uneven
Through a rank wilderness of fern and flower;
She judged petals in disarray,
The whole season, sloven.

How she longed for winter then!—
Scrupulously austere in its order
Of white and black
Ice and rock; each sentiment within border,
And heart's frosty discipline
Exact as a snowflake.

But here—a burgeoning
Unruly enough to pitch her five queenly wits
Into vulgar motley—
A treason not to be borne; let idiots
Reel giddy in bedlam spring;
She withdrew neatly.

And round her house she set
Such a barricade of barb and check
Against mutinous weather
As no mere insurgent man could hope to break
With curse, fist, threat
Or love, either.

*Sylvia Plath (1932-63)*

# FINALE

All my life I have struggled from gentleness
And men. Shaking off heatsteam
From the far, dry corners of desire. Kissing only
Where, in wet smooth black alleyways, the crows
Pack hunting in crowds.
And here, at the end of the tape, I feel sun
Beating on my shoulders like a light
And warm. To trust and kiss and love you
In clasping beauty. Teach me of
Wonderful silences, far in the glowing
Of your eyes, my tears.
Let my passion kill me.

*Sue Lenier (b.1957)*

## BODY LANGUAGE

He loved her so he wrote
a long, passionate poem, melting
his heart's wax on the page all night,
burning the wick of his words at all ends
to attract her.
She loved him and her little cries
opened and closed like night anemones,
scenting the empty air
with the witching words of her mouth
to call him to her.
Neither came to the other.
All night long he held himself spell-
bound in the small circle of his own light
until he was burnt out,
and she, mesmerized by her own charms,
entered the flower of herself
and drew in her arms.


*Sylvia Kantaris (b.1936)*

# NARCISSUS

What he liked in her voice
was his name
called over & over
and the mirrorlike look
in the weeping eyes of his lover;
in the end, left her
on a chill mountain shelf,
in a damp cave
with her wits and her words astray,
to devote himself
to himself.

Then the gods with indolent yawns
took a high hand with him for
such eNOR
mous self-love
was considered by others a bore.

Changed to a flower
he stood by the river
a sad case
of rooted vanity;
he never forgave
the reflecting water
for rippling his face.

*Gerda Mayer (b.1927)*

## AT A RECEPTION

Now I am glad to be one whom people ignore:
none except we know that you have singled me out.
Shaking hands as if you had not kissed my eyes,
exchanging memories of touch, let go before
others can see you making me become
the most exciting woman in the room.

*Karen Gershon (b.1923)*

## FROM THE TELEPHONE

Out of the dark cup
Your voice broke like a flower.
It trembled, swaying on its taut stem.
The caress in its touch
Made my eyes close.

*Florence Ripley Mastin (late 19th/early 20th century)*

# VILLEGGIATURE

My window, framed in pear-tree bloom,
White-curtained shone, and softly lighted:
So, by the pear-tree, to my room
Your ghost last night climbed uninvited.

Your solid self, long leagues away,
Deep in dull books, had hardly missed me;
And yet you found this Romeo's way,
And through the blossom climbed and kissed me.

I watched the still and dewy lawn,
The pear-tree boughs hung white above you;
I listened to you till the dawn,
And half forgot I did not love you.

Oh, dear! what pretty things you said,
What pearls of song you threaded for me!
I did not—till your ghost had fled—
Remember how you always bore me!

*Edith Nesbit (1858-1924)*

# UNFORTUNATE COINCIDENCE

By the time you swear you're his,
Shivering and sighing,
And he vows his passion is
Infinite, undying—
Lady, make a note of this:
One of you is lying.

*Dorothy Parker (1893-1967)*

# FROM THE GARDEN

Come, my beloved,
consider the lilies.
We are of little faith.
We talk too much.
Put your mouthful of words away
and come with me to watch
the lilies open in such a field,
growing there like yachts,
slowly steering their petals
without nurses or clocks.
Let us consider the view:
a house where white clouds
decorate the muddy halls.
Oh, put away your good words
and your bad words. Spit out
your words like stones!
Come here! Come here!
Come eat my pleasant fruits.

*Anne Sexton (1928-74)*

# OPEN SECRETS

Because you are beautiful I will have to tell you a number
    of my secrets.
(What does anyone hide anything for except to have it
    found?)

I have concealed from you too long the fact that space
    is curved,
That I have invented the night the better to see you by,
    that
If I seem upset at times it is because of the way you walk,
    leaning into wind,

That most of my secrets are doors that open onto other
    secrets—
(Vistas of fields and beaches and columns stretching on
    forever),

That even these words are secrets with turquoise doors
    in them,
Opening out to one side or the other, letting you glimpse
    for two seconds
Herds of speaking horses, temples full of starfish,
    clandestine moons,

And as you walk, leaning into wind, into the terrible landscape
    of your own beauty,
These secrets are my gifts to you, these signs that lead you
    to my door.

*Gwendolyn MacEwen (1941-87)*

# TO SPEAK OF MY INFLUENCES

To speak of my influences:
Above all, your eyes,
And next, that jar of the bell
When I think it is you who call.
Since half the time it is not,
I have fevers to quell.
To speak as well
Of the rain in the night
We suddenly heard lying there,
That satin'd stress of a crazy wine
Silverly beating down.
That music, too, you played—
Or was it your elan,
Dense and rich? A sea-clashed mist
Warred with the wracked pulse
That danced my blood to flame
Plagued by certain notes
Of irritable brilliance and flutes
Velvet-mouthed. Ah, monotone
Of phrases faded into dissolution!
Dazed, credulous, I lived
Unbalanced by such powers
As ruled me like that speech you played
And rain's metallic waterfalls.
They ruled me, yes. Eyes kissed my eyes
And ears stunned by the delicacy
Of that fire-in-the-straw art
Wished no more than to be
Set once more alight.

To speak of my influences:
By force of fate, you said,
Who came with masks, imported more
When the suave cords were twanged,
Increased the speed at which it wound
Its flaunting silk of sound.
O heresy! All changes
Save this art at which we play,
The instant, drenched in rain,
We imitated once again
But have we the cunning to
Keep enthrallment vivid?

Straw-in-the-fire love,
It's no morality play we're in,
Nor can we trick time
Nor end where we began.
Let us end as we will
While I make apostrophes
That will not more excel
Than your eyes, our dance,
And we'll love on by chance.


*Jean Garrigue (b.1914)*

# HYMN TO EROS

O Eros, silently smiling one, hear me.
Let the shadow of thy wings
brush me.
Let thy presence
enfold me, as if darkness
were swandown.
Let me see that darkness
lamp in hand,
this country become
the other country
sacred to desire.

Drowsy god,
slow the wheels of my thought
so that I listen only
to the snowfall hush of
thy circling.
Close my beloved with me
in the smoke ring of thy power,
that we may be, each to the other,
figures of flame,
figures of smoke,
figures of flesh
newly seen in the dusk.

*Denise Levertov (b.1923)*

## FIRE US WITH ICE,
## BURN US WITH SNOW

As *Corydon* went shiv'ring by,
*Sylvia* a Ball of Snow let fly,
Which straight a Globe of Fire became,
And put the Shepherd in a Flame;
*Cupid* now break thy Darts and Bow,
*Sylvia* can all thy Feats out-do,
Fire us with Ice, burn us with Snow.

*Mary Monk (c.1677–1715)*

# TO MY HEAVENLY CHARMER

My poor expecting Heart beats for thy Breast,
In ev'ry Pulse, and will not let me rest;
A thousand dear Desires are waking there,
Whose Softness will not a Description bear,
Oh! let me pour them to thy lovely Eyes,
And catch their tender Meanings as they rise.
My ev'ry Feature with my Passion glows
In ev'ry Thought and Look it overflows.
Too noble and too strong for all Disguise,
It rushes from my Love-discov'ring Eyes.
Nor Rules nor Reason can my Love restrain;
Its godlike Tide runs high in ev'ry Vein.
To the whole World my Tenderness be known,
What is the World to her, who lives for thee alone.

*Martha Sansom (1690-1736)*

## PROPHETIC SOUL

Because your eyes are slant and slow,
Because your hair is sweet to touch,
My heart is high again; but oh,
I doubt if this will get me much.

*Dorothy Parker (1893-1967)*

# From PASSION

i
He draws memory out of me with hands of fire.
His touch is miracle and shock.

My masseur strokes me into swallow-light,
torrents of dove.

He kneads me. His fingers are wildfire and blush,
rose and scorch. I bask and singe. His hands burn me.

I moan. He firms the fiery earth of me.
He sears the air of me. My flesh furnaces.
(But his kiss on my throat pulses a cool radish scent.)

We loll and sweat on his plush throne, on far-flung cushions.
I tremble under the tact of his touch.

His tongue floods me like honey and cirrus.
I slide into my own sheet-of-fire ghost.


ii
Like a god humming and making things
he puts his lips against mine. Oh I shiver!
I freeze! He is ice. He is knife-bladed and bleak-beaked lover.

Now I am his oblong silk scarf left to chill in the freezer,
along with the icecream and the raspberries stelled with frost.

He is frost-bite.
He kisses each nipple to zero.
His sex is a prism of ice in me.

Now the sky calls out for its birds in my voice.
Now a door of dawn slams.

Our reign of henna and sauna is over.
He flies to heaven on my warm heart.


*Penelope Shuttle (b.1947)*

# ATTRACTION

The meadow and the mountain with desire
    Gazed on each other, till a fierce unrest
    Surged 'neath the meadow's seemingly calm breast,
And all the mountain's fissures ran with fire.

A mighty river rolled between them there.
    What could the mountain do but gaze and burn?
    What could the meadow do but look and yearn,
And gem its bosom to conceal despair?

Their seething passion agitated space,
    Till lo! the lands a sudden earthquake shook,
    The river fled: the meadow leaped, and took
The leaning mountain in a close embrace.

*Ella Wheeler Wilcox (1850-1919)*

## TWO SONGS

Sex, as they harshly call it,
I fell into this morning
at ten o'clock, a drizzling hour
of traffic and wet newspapers.
I thought of him who yesterday
clearly didn't
turn me to a hot field
ready for plowing,
and longing for that young man
piercéd me to the roots
bathing every vein, etc.
All day he appears to me
touchingly desirable,
a prize one could wreck one's peace for.
I'd call it love if love
didn't take so many years
but lust too is a jewel
a sweet flower and what
pure happiness to know
all our high-toned questions
breed in a lively animal.
That "old last act"!
And yet sometimes
all seems post coitum triste
and I a mere bystander.
Somebody else is going off,
getting shot to the moon.

Or, a moon-race!
Split seconds after
my opposite number lands
I make it—
we lie fainting together
at a crater-edge
heavy as mercury in our moonsuits
till he speaks—
in a different language
yet one I've picked up
through cultural exchanges . . .
we murmur the first moonwords:
*Spasibo. Thanks. O.K.*


*Adrienne Rich (b.1929)*

# THE DISAPPOINTMENT

One day the Amorous *Lysander*,
By an impatient Passion sway'd,
Surpriz'd fair *Cloris*, that lov'd Maid,
Who could defend her self no longer.
All things did with his Love conspire;
The gilded Planet of the Day,
In his gay Chariot drawn by Fire,
Was now descending to the Sea,
And left no Light to guide the World,
But what from *Cloris* Brighter Eyes was hurl'd.

In a lone Thicket made for Love,
Silent as yielding Maids Consent,
She with a Charming Languishment,
Permits his Force, yet gently strove;
Her Hands his Bosom softly meet,
But not to put him back design'd,
Rather to draw 'em on inclin'd:
Whilst he lay trembling at her Feet,
Resistance 'tis in vain to show;
She wants the pow'r to say—*Ah! What d'ye do?*

Her Bright Eyes sweet, and yet severe,
Where Love and Shame confus'dly strive,
Fresh Vigor to *Lysander* give;
And breathing faintly in his Ear,
She cry'd—*Cease, Cease—your vain Desire,*
*Or I'll call out—What would you do?*
*My Dearer Honour ev'n to You*
*I cannot, must not give—Retire,*
*Or take this Life, whose chiefest part*
*I gave you with the Conquest of my Heart.*

But he as much unus'd to Fear,
As he was capable of Love,
The blessed minutes to improve,
Kisses her Mouth, her Neck, her Hair;
Each Touch her new Desire Alarms.
His burning trembling Hand he prest
Upon her swelling Snowy Brest,
While she lay panting in his Arms.
All her Unguarded Beauties lie
The Spoils and Trophies of the Energy.

Her balmy lips countring his,
As their Souls, are joyn'd;
Both in Transports Unconfin'd
Extend themselves upon the Moss.
*Cloris* half dead and breathless lay;
Her soft Eyes cast a Humid Light,
Such as divides the Day and Night;
Or falling Stars, whose Fires decay:
And now no signs of Life she shows,
But what in short breath'd Sighs returns and goes.

He saw how at her length she lay;
He saw her rising Bosom bare;
Her loose thin *Robes*, through which appear
A Shape design'd for Love and Play;
Abandon'd by her Pride and Shame.
She does her softest Joys dispence,
Off'ring her Virgin-Innocence
A Victim to Loves Sacred Flame;
While the o'er-Ravish'd Shepherd lies
Unable to perform the Sacrifice.

Ready to taste a thousand Joys,
The too transported hapless Swain
Found the vast Pleasure turn'd to Pain;
Pleasure which too much Love destroys:
The willing Garments by he laid,
And Heaven all open'd to his view,
Mad to possess, himself he threw
On the Defenceless Lovely Maid.
But Oh what envying God conspires
To snatch his Power, yet leave him the Desire.

*Nature's Support,* (without whose Aid
She can no Humane Being give)
It self now wants the Art to live;
Faintness its slack'ned Nerves invade:
In vain th'inraged Youth essay'd
To call its fleeting Vigor back,
No motion 'twill from Motion take;
Excess of Love is Love betray'd:
In vain he Toils, in vain Commands,
Then I sensible fell weeping in his Hand.

In this so Amorous Cruel Strife,
Where Love and Fate were too severe
The poor *Lysander* in despair
Renounc'd his Reason with his Life
Now all the brisk and active Fire
That should the Nobler Part inflame,
Serv'd to increase his Rage and Shame
And left no Spark for New Desire:
Not all her Naked Charms cou'd move
Or calm that Rage that had debauch'd his Love.

*Cloris* returning from the Trance
Which Love and soft Desire had bred,
Her timerous Hand she gently laid
(Or guided by Design or Chance)
Soon that Fabulous *Priapus*,
That Potent God, as Poets feign;
But never did young *Shepherdess*,
Gath'ring of Fern upon the Plain,
Nimbly draw her Fingers back,
Finding beneath the verdant Leaves a Snake.

*Aphra Behn (1640-89)*

# POEM FOR SIGMUND

It's a funny thing,
a Brontosaurus with a long neck
and pea-sized brain, only room
for one thought and that's
not extinction. It's lucky
its mouth is vertical
and not the other way
or we'd see it
smiling like a Cheshire cat.
(Hard to get in the mood
with that grin in your mind.)
No wonder I feel fond of it,
its simple trust of me
as my hands slide down your belly,
the way it jumps up
like a drawing in a child's pop-up book,
expecting me
to say "Hi!
Surprised to see you,"
expecting tenderness
from these envious woman's hands.


*Lorna Crozier (b.1948)*

# THE CONNOISSEUSE OF SLUGS

When I was a connoisseuse of slugs
I would part the ivy leaves, and look for the
naked jelly of those gold bodies,
translucent strangers glistening along the
stones, slowly, their gelatinous bodies
at my mercy. Made mostly of water, they would shrivel
to nothing if they were sprinkled with salt,
but I was not interested in that. What I liked
was to draw aside the ivy, breathe the
odor of the wall, and stand there in silence
until the slug forgot I was there
and sent its antennae up out of its
head, the glimmering umber horns
rising like telescopes, until finally the sensitive knobs would
pop out the ends,
delicate and intimate. Years later,
when I first saw a naked man,
I gasped with pleasure to see that quiet
mystery reenacted, the slow
elegant being coming out of hiding and
gleaming in the dark air, eager and so
trusting you could weep.

*Sharon Olds*

# THE OLD MAN

Often after we make love
I dream of your agèd father
as if our lovemaking
has led back to your beginning,
your sire roused by our pleasure.
In the vigour of his age
he's like an old charioteer
telling us that what we ride on
is our life,
what we use as our vehicle
is the breath
one day we will let go of forever
as for an instant
we let go of it in love.

*Penelope Shuttle (b.1947)*

# THE AVENUE

Who has not seen their lover
Walking at ease,
Walking like any other
A pavement under trees,
Not singular, apart,
But footed, featured, dressed,
Approaching like the rest
In the same dapple of the summer caught;
Who has not suddenly thought
With swift surprise:
There walks in cool disguise,
There comes, my heart.

*Frances Cornford (1886-1960)*

# I MUST BE ABLE TO PROTECT YOU

i
I must be able to protect you.
Protecting you is my protection
from myself.

ii
The wall I have built around myself from
the world,
does not allow   even you   to penetrate.
If you want to come in
through the wall
that I have built   around you   you must
enter, through me.

*'Marnia'* (1968-92)

# LOVING YOU

soft as old silk
I tread in this room
wary of space
that between us flows
you know me
as fish knows fish in tide—
no more you know
I could mark you through to the bone—
no touch
you'd own
so gently I walk
around the space
enclosing you
soft as silk
loving you

*Frances Horovitz (1938-83)*

# THE KISS

The snow is white on wood and wold,
  The wind is in the firs,
So dead my heart is with the cold,
  No pulse within it stirs,
Even to see your face, my dear,
  Your face that was my sun;
There is no spring this bitter year,
  And summer's dreams are done.

The snakes that lie about my heart
  Are in their wintry sleep;
Their fangs no more deal sting and smart,
  No more they curl and creep.
Love with the summer ceased to be;
  The frost is firm and fast.
God keep the summer far from me,
  And let the snakes' sleep last!

Touch of your hand could not suffice
  To waken them once more;
Nor could the sunshine of your eyes
  A ruined spring restore.
But ah—your lips! You know the rest:
  The snows are summer rain,
My eyes are wet, and in my breast
  The snakes' fangs meet again.

*Edith Nesbit (1858-1924)*

## OH, HOW THE HAND THE LOVER
## OUGHT TO PRIZE

Oh, how the hand the lover ought to prize
    'Bove any one peculiar grace!
While he is dying for the eyes
    And doting on the lovely face,
The unconsid'ring little knows
How much he to this beauty owes.

That, when the lover absent is,
    Informs him of his mistress' heart;
'Tis that which gives him all his bliss
    When dear love-secrets 'twill impart:
That plights the faith the maid bestows,
And that confirms the tim'rous vows.

'Tis that betrays the tenderness
    Which the too bashful tongue denies;
'Tis that which does the heart confess,
    And spares the language of the eyes;
'Tis that which treasure gives so vast,
Ev'n Iris 'twill to Damon give at last.

*Aphra Behn (1640-89)*

# LOVE-POEM

Yours is the face that the earth turns to me—
Continuous beyond its human features, lie
The mountain forms that rest against the sky.
With your eyes, the reflecting rainbow, the sun's light
Sees me; forest and flowers, bird and beast
Know and hold me for ever in the world's thought,
Creation's deep untroubled retrospect.

When your hand touches mine, it is the earth
That takes me—the deep grass,
And rocks and rivers, the green graves,
And children still unborn, and ancestors,
In love passed down from hand to hand from God.
Your touch comes from the creation of the world,
From those paternal fingers streaming through the clouds
That break with light the surface of the sea.

Here, where I trace your body with my hand
Love's presence has no end;
For these, your arms that hold me, are the world's.
In us, the continents clouds and oceans meet
Our arbitrary selves, extensive with the night,
Lost in the heart's worship and the body's sleep.

*Kathleen Raine (b.1908)*

# A LYNMOUTH WIDOW

He was straight and strong, and his eyes were blue
As the summer meeting of sky and sea,
And the ruddy cliffs had a colder hue
Than flushed his cheek when he married me.

We passed the porch where the swallows breed,
We left the little brown church behind,
And I leaned on his arm, though I had no need,
Only to feel him so strong and kind.

One thing I never can quite forget;
It grips my throat when I try to pray—
The keen salt smell of a drying net
That hung on the churchyard wall that day.

He would have taken a long, long grave—
A long, long grave, for he stood so tall . . .
Oh, God, the crash of a breaking wave,
And the smell of the nets on the churchyard wall!

*Amelia Josephine Burr (late 19th/early 20th century)*

# DOUGLAS, DOUGLAS, TENDER AND TRUE

Could you come back to me, Douglas, Douglas,
In the old likeness that I knew,
I would be so faithful, so loving, Douglas,
Douglas, Douglas, tender and true.

Never a scornful word should grieve ye,
I'd smile on ye sweet as the angels do;—
Sweet as your smile on me shone ever,
Douglas, Douglas, tender and true.

Oh, to call back the days that are not!
My eyes were blinded, your words were few;
Do you know the truth now up in heaven,
Douglas, Douglas, tender and true?

I never was worthy of you, Douglas;
Not half worthy the like of you:
Now all men beside seem to me like shadows—
I love you, Douglas, tender and true.

Stretch out your hand to me, Douglas, Douglas,
Drop forgiveness from heaven like dew;
As I lay my heart on your dead heart, Douglas,
Douglas, Douglas, tender and true.


*Dinah Maria Craik  (1826-87)*

# THE SILLER CROUN

And ye shall walk in silk attire,
    And siller hae to spare,
Gin ye'll consent to be his bride,
    Nor think o' Donald mair.
O wha wad buy a silken goun
    Wi' a poor broken heart!
Or what's to me a siller croun,
    Gin frae my love I part!

The mind wha's every wish is pure
    Far dearer is to me;
And ere I'm forc'd to break my faith,
    I'll lay me down an' dee!
For I hae pledg'd my virgin troth
    Brave Donald's fate to share;
And he has gi'en to me his heart,
    Wi' a' its virtues rare.

His gentle manners wan my heart,
    He gratefu' took the gift;
Could I but think to seek it back,
    It wad be waur than theft!
For langest life can ne'er repay
    The love he bears to me;
And ere I'm forc'd to break my troth,
    I'll lay me doun an' dee.

*Susanna Blamire (1747-94)*

# THOSE WHO LOVE

Those who love the most,
Do not talk of their love,
Francesca, Guinevere,
Deirdre, Iseult, Heloise,
In the fragrant gardens of heaven
Are silent, or speak if at all
Of fragile inconsequent things.

And a woman I used to know
Who loved one man from her youth,
Against the strength of the fates
Fighting in somber pride
Never spoke of this thing,
But hearing his name by chance,
A light would pass over her face.

*Sara Teasdale (1884–1933)*

## From LAST TESTAMENTS

Before she walked into the river
and didn't come back,
the woman who couldn't remember
the day of the week
or the faces of her children,
made a list of all the men
she'd ever loved,
left it for her husband by the coffee pot,
his name on the bottom,
underlined twice
for emphasis.

*Lorna Crozier (b.1948)*

## LOVE'S ADVOCATE

I remember sitting together in parks
leaning over bridges
counting trout and swans
holding hands under arches
kissing away suns
and moons into darkness.

I remember platform good-byes
last-minute trains
slamming us apart
and my non-self walking back alone.
I remember smaller things:
a pebble in my shoe
and you throwing a match-box on the Serpentine.

I stood still hearing the years
flow over and over
as over a stone
in a river-bed
polishing, cleaning, wearing away.
But I still remember the last day.

What I cannot remember is how I felt—
mind, love's advocate,
must remind heart
of the end, the abyss.
The bottom of the world remains;
each day climbs to a new start.

*Phoebe Hesketh (b.1909)*

# WINTER

The tree still bends over the lake,
And I try to recall our love,
Our love which had a thousand leaves.

*Sheila Wingfield (1906-92)*

# TO MY HUSBAND

When from the world, I shall be tane,
And from earths necessary paine,
Then let no blacks be worne for me,
Not in a Ring my dear by thee.
But this bright Diamond, let it be
Worn in rememberance of me.
And when it sparkles in your eye,
Think 'tis my shadow passeth by.
For why, more bright you shall me see,
Then that or any Gem can bee.
Dress not the house with sable weed,
As if there was some dismal deed
Acted to be when I am gone,
There is no cause for me to mourn.
And let no badge of Herald be
The sign of my Antiquity.
It was my glory I did spring
From heavens eternall powerful King:
To his bright Palace heir am I.
It is his promise, hee'l not lye.
By my dear Brother lay me,
It was a promise made by thee,
And now I must bid thee adieu,
For I'me a parting now from you.

*'Eliza'* (fl. c. 1652)

# REMEMBER

Remember me when I am gone away,
Gone far away into the silent land;
When you can no more hold me by the hand,
Nor I half turn to go yet turning stay.
Remember me when no more day by day
You tell me of our future that you planned:
Only remember me; you understand
It will be late to counsel then or pray.
Yet if you should forget me for a while
And afterwards remember, do not grieve:
For if the darkness and corruption leave
A vestige of the thoughts that once I had,
Better by far you should forget and smile
Than that you should remember and be sad.

*Christina Rossetti (1830-94)*

# ECHO

Come to me in the silence of the night;
    Come in the speaking silence of a dream;
Come with soft rounded cheeks and eyes as bright
    As sunlight on a stream;
        Come back in tears,
O memory, hope, love of finished years.

Oh dream how sweet, too sweet, too bitter sweet,
    Whose wakening should have been in Paradise,
Where souls brimfull of love abide and meet;
    Where thirsting longing eyes
        Watch the slow door
That opening, letting in, lets out no more.

Yet come to m e in dreams, that I may live
    My very life again tho' cold in death:
Come back to me in dreams, that I may give
    Pulse for pulse, breath for breath:
        Speak low, lean low,
As long ago, my love, how long ago.

*Christina Rossetti (1830-94)*

# From UPON THE DEATH OF HER HUSBAND

Yet, gentle shade! whether thou now does rove,
Thro' some blest vale, or ever verdant grove,
One moment listen to my grief and take
The softest vows that ever love can make.
For thee, all thoughts of pleasure I forgo,
For thee, my tears shall never cease to flow;
For thee at once I from the world retire,
To feed in silent shades a hopeless fire.
My bosom all thy image shall retain,
The full impression there shall still remain
As thou has taught my tender heart to prove
The noblest height and elegance of love,
That sacred passion I to thee confine.
My spotless faith shall be for ever thine.

*Elizabeth Singer Rowe (1674-1737)*

# WERENA MY HEART LICHT I WAD DEE

There was ance a may, and she lo'ed na men;
She biggit\* her bonnie bow'r doun i' yon glen;     \*built
But now she cries, Dool and a well-a-day!
Come doun the green gait\* and come here away!      \*way

When bonnie young Johnnie cam' owre the sea
He said he saw naething sae lovely as me;
He hecht\* me baith rings and monie braw things; \*promised
And werena my heart licht, I wad dee.

He had a wee tittie\* that lo'ed na me,                \*sister
Because I was twice as bonnie as she;
She raised sic a pother 'twixt him and his mother,
That werena my heart licht, I wad dee.

The day it was set, and the bridal to be
The wife took a dwam\* and lay doun to dee;       \*swoon
She maned, and she graned, out o' dolour and pain,
Till he vowed that he ne'er wad see me again.

His kin was for ane o' a higher degree,
Said, what had he do wi' the likes o' me?
Albeit I was bonnie, I wasna for Johnnie:
And werena my heart licht, I wad dee.

They said I had neither cow nor calf,
Nor dribbles o' drink rins through the draff,\*       \*grain
Nor pickles o' meal rins through the mill-e'e;
And werena my heart licht, I wad dee.

His tittie she was baith wily and slee,
She spied me as I cam' owre the lea,
And then she ran in and made a loud din;
Believe your ain een an ye trow na me.

His bannet stood aye fu' round on his brow
His auld ane looked aye as weel as some's new;
But now he lets 't wear ony gate it will hing,
And casts himsel' dowie upon the corn-bing.

And now he gaes daund'ring about the dykes
And a' he dow* do is to hund the tykes;          *can
The love-lang nicht he ne'er steeks* his e'e;    *closes
And werena my heart licht I wad dee.

Were I but young for thee, as I ha'e been
We should ha'e been gallopin' doun in yon green,
And linkin' it* on the lily-white lea;          *going arm
And wow, gin I were but young for thee.              in arm

*Grizel Baillie (1665-1746)*

# SONG

Why *Damon*, why, why, why so pressing?
The Heart you beg's not worth possessing:
Each Look, each Word, each Smile's affected,
And inward Charms are quite neglected:
    Then scorn her, scorn her, foolish Swain,
    And sigh no more, no more in vain.

Beauty's worthless, fading, flying;
Who would for Trifles think of dying?
Who for a Face, a Shape, wou'd languish,
And tell the Brooks, and Groves his Anguish,
    Till she, till she thinks fit to prize him,
    And all, and all beside despise him?

Fix, fix your Thoughts on what's inviting,
On what will never bear the slighting:
Wit and Virtue claim your Duty,
They're much more worth than Gold and Beauty:
    To them, to them, your Heart resign,
    And you'll no more, no more repine.

*Mary Chudleigh (1656-1710)*

# BETWEEN YOUR SHEETS

Between your sheets you soundly sleep
Nor dream of vigils that we lovers keep
While all the night, I waking sigh your name,
The tender sound does every nerve inflame,
Imagination shows me all your charms,
The plenteous silken hair, and waxen arms,
The well turned neck, and snowy rising breast
And all the beauties that supinely rest
          between your sheets.

Ah Lindamira, could you see my heart,
How fond, how true, how free from fraudful art,
The warmest glances poorly do explain
The eager wish, the melting throbbing pain
Which through my very blood and soul I feel,
Which you cannot believe nor I reveal,
Which every metaphor must render less
And yet (methinks) which I could well express
          between your sheets.

*Lady Mary Wortley Montagu (1689-1762)*

## A MAN IN LOVE

*L'Homme qui ne se trouve point &*
*ne se trouvera jamais*

The man who feels the dear disease,
Forgets himself, neglects to please:
The crowd avoids and seeks the groves,
And much he thinks when much he loves;
Press'd with alternate hope and fear,
Sighs in her absence, sighs when she is near.
The gay, the fond, the fair, the young,
Those trifles pass unseen along;
To him a pert, insipid throng.
But most he shuns the vain coquet;
Contemns her false affected wit:
The minstrels sound, the flowing bowl
Oppress and hurt the am'rous soul.
'Tis solitude alone can please,
And give some intervals of ease.
He feeds the soft distemper there,
And fondly courts the distant fair;
To balls, the silent shade prefers,
And hates all other charms but hers.
When thus your absent swain can do,
Molly, you may believe him true.

*Lady Mary Wortley Montagu (1689-1762)*

# MARY'S SONG

I wad ha'e gi'en him my lips tae kiss,
Had I been his, had I been his;
Barely breid and elder wine,
Had I been his as he is mine.

The wanderin' bee it seeks the rose;
Tae the lochan's bosom the burnie goes;
The grey bird cries at evenin's fa',
'My luve, my fair one, come awa'.'

My beloved sall ha'e this he'rt tae break,
Reid, reid wine and the barley cake.
A he'rt tae break, and a mou' tae kiss,
Tho' he be nae mine, as I am his.


*Marion Angus (1866-1946)*

# AH ME, IF I GREW SWEET TO MAN

Ah me, if I grew sweet to man
It was but as a rose that can
No longer keep the breath that heaves
And swells among its folded leaves.

The pressing fragrance would unclose
The flower, and I become a rose,
That unimpeachable and fair
Planted its sweetness in the air.

No art I used men's love to draw;
I lived but by my being's law,
As roses are by heaven designed
To bring the honey to the wind.

*Michael Field (1846-1914 & 1862-1913)*

# From YOUTH AND MAIDENHOOD

Like a drop of water is my heart
    Laid upon her soft and rosy palm,
Turned whichever way her hand doth turn,
    Trembling in an ecstasy of calm.

Like a broken rose-leaf is my heart,
    Held within her close and burning clasp,
Breathing only dying sweetness out,
    Withering beneath the fatal grasp.

Like a vapoury cloudlet is my heart,
    Growing into beauty near the sun,
Gaining rainbow hues in her embrace,
    Melting into tears when it is done.

Like mine own dear harp is this my heart,
    Dumb, without the hand that sweeps its strings;
Though the hand be careless or be cruel,
    When it comes, my heart breaks forth and sings.


*Sarah Williams (1841-68)*

# SONG

Nothing ades to Loves fond fire
More then scorn and cold disdain
I to cherish your desire
kindness used but twas in vain
you insulted on your Slave
To be mine you soon refused
Hope hope not then the power to have
Which ingloriously you used
Thinke not Thersis I will ere
By my love my Empire loose
you grow Constant through dispare
kindness you would soon abuse
Though you still possess my hart
Scorn and rigor I must fain
there remaines noe other art
your Love fond fugitive to gain

*Elizabeth Wilmot (d.1681)*

# I WILL NOT GIVE THEE
# ALL MY HEART

I will not give thee all my heart
For that I need a place apart
To dream my dreams in, and I know
Few sheltered ways for dreams to go:
But when I shut the door upon
Some secret wonder—still, withdrawn—
Why does thou love me even more,
And hold me closer than before?

When I of love demand the least,
Thou biddest him to fire and feast:
When I am hungry and would eat,
There is no bread, though crusts were sweet.
If I with manna may be fed,
Shall I go all uncomforted?
Nay! Howsoever dear thou art,
I will not give thee all my heart.

*Grace Hazard Conkling (late 19th/early 20th century)*

# THE LOVER: A BALLAD

At length, by so much importunity pressed,
Take, C—, at once the inside of my breast;
This stupid indiff'rence so often you blame,
Is not owing to nature, to fear, or to shame;
I am not as cold as a virgin in lead,
Nor is Sunday's sermon so strong in my head:
I know but too well how Time flies along,
That we live but few years, and yet fewer are young.

But I hate to be cheated, and never will buy
Long years of repentance for moments of joy.
Oh! was there a man (but where shall I find
Good sense and good nature so equally joined?)
Would value his pleasure, contribute to mine;
Not meanly would boast, nor would lewdly design;
Not over severe, yet not stupidly vain,
For I would have the power, tho' not give the pain.

No pedant, yet learnèd; no rake-helly gay,
Or laughing, because he has nothing to say;
To all my whole sex obliging and free,
Yet never be fond of any but me;
In public preserve the decorum that's just,
And shew in his eyes he is true to his trust;
Then rarely approach, and respectfully bow,
But not fulsomely pert, nor yet foppishly low.

But when the long hours of public are past,
And we meet with champagne and a chicken at last,
May ev'ry fond pleasure that moment endear;
Be banished afar both discretion and fear!
Forgetting or scorning the airs of the crowd,
He may cease to be formal, and I to be proud,
'Till lost in the joy we confess that we live,
And he may be rude, and yet I may forgive.

And that my delight may be solidly fixed,
Let the friend and the lover be handsomely mixed;
In whose tender bosom my soul may confide,
Whose kindness can sooth me, whose counsel can guide.
From such a dear lover as here I describe,
No danger should fright me, no millions should bribe;
But till this astonishing creature I know,
As I long have lived chaste, I will keep myself so.

I never will share with the wanton coquet,
Or be caught by a vain affectation of wit.
The toasters and songsters may try all their art,
But never shall enter the pass of my heart.
I loathe the lewd rake, the dressed fopling despise:
Before such pursuers the nice virgin flies:
And as Ovid has sweetly in parable told,
We harden like trees, and like rivers grow cold.

*Lady Mary Wortley Montagu (1689-1762)*

# EVE-SONG

I span and Eve span
A thread to bind the heart of man;
But the heart of man was a wandering thing
That came and went with little to bring:
Nothing he minded what we made,
As here he loitered, and there he stayed.

I span and Eve span
A thread to bind the heart of man;
But the more we span the more we found
It wasn't his heart but ours we bound.
For children gathered about our knees:
The thread was a chain that stole our ease.
And one of us learned in our children's eyes
That more than man was love and prize.
But deep in the heart of one of us lay
A root of loss and hidden dismay.

He said he was strong. He had no strength
But that which comes of breadth and length.
He said he was fond. But his fondness proved
The flame of an hour when he was moved.
He said he was true. His truth was but
A door that winds could open and shut.

And yet, and yet, as he came back,
Wandering in from the outward track,
We held our arms, and gave him our breast,
As a pillowing place for his head to rest.
I span and Eve span,
A thread to bind the heart of man!

*Mary Gilmore (1865-1962)*

# THE HUMBLE WISH

I ask not wit, nor beauty do I crave,
Nor wealth, nor pompous titles wish to have;
But since 'tis doom'd, in all degrees of life,
(Whether a daughter, sister, or a wife,)
That females shall the stronger males obey,
And yield perforce to their tyrannic sway;
Since this, I say, is every woman's fate,
Give me a mind to suit my slavish state.

*Mrs. B-LL M-RT-N (fl. c.1726)*

# O DONALD! YE ARE JUST THE MAN

O Donald! ye are just the man
    Who, when he's got a wife,
Begins to fratch—nae notice ta'en—
    They're strangers a' their life.

The fan may drop—she takes it up,
    The husband keeps his chair;
She hands the kettle—gives his cup—
    Without e'en—"thank ye, dear."

Now, truly, these slights are but toys;
    But frae neglects like these,
The wife may soon a slattern grow,
    And strive nae mair to please.

For wooers ay do all they can
    To trifle wi' the mind;
They hold the blaze of beauty up,
    And keep the poor things blind.

But wedlock tears away the veil,
    The goddess is nae mair;
He thinks his wife a silly thing,
    She thinks her man a bear.

Let then the lover be the friend—
    The loving friend for life;
Think but thysel the happiest spouse,
    She'll be the happiest wife.

*Susanna Blamire (1747-94)*

# ADVICE TO HER SON ON MARRIAGE

from *The Conclusion of a Letter to the Rev. Mr C—*


When you gain her Affection, take care to preserve it;
Lest others persuade her, you do not deserve it.
Still study to heighten the Joys of her Life;
Not treat her the worse, for her being your Wife.
If in Judgment she errs, set her right, without Pride:
'Tis the Province of insolent Fools, to deride.
A Husband's first Praise, is a *Friend* and *Protector*:
Then change not these Titles, for *Tyrant* and *Hector*.
Let your Person be neat, unaffectedly clean,
Tho' alone with your wife the whole Day you remain.
Chuse Books, for her study, to fashion her Mind,
To emulate those who excell'd of her Kind.
Be Religion the principal Care of your Life,
As you hope to be blest in your Children and Wife:
So you, in your Marriage, shall gain its true End;
And find, in your Wife, a *Companion* and *Friend*.


*Mary Barber (c.1690-1757)*

# DOUBLE BED

She goes upstairs early,
lies wretched in the double bed,
letting its cool space ease her.
The curtains strain a thin daylight.
People move faintly beneath.

Tired out, she enters soon
those inner vastnesses
where wishes are almost naked,
pursuing new shapes
of desire, new solitudes.

She wakes fractiously
as the bed rearranges its sinews
for a heavier transport.
He brings her cold flesh
and delicate flattery:

and at length she plays her part,
breathless, half-drowning,
while he straddles her as if
he would life-save her.
He's not a brute;

she's not all innocence.
It's just that, by daylight,
they inhabit different angles,
no longer wave and smile
from each other's mirrors.

So, not unkindly,
he turns his back
(he can never sleep facing her)
and she will lie staring
at the dark for hours,

motionless, disarrayed
in the space he has left her.
It is too narrow to sleep in,
but impossible to leave,
she thinks, without robbing
him.

*Carol Rumens (b.1944)*

# THE DISAPPOINTED WIFE

The ardent lover cannot find
A coldness in his fair unkind;
But, blaming what he cannot hate,
He mildly chides the dear ingrate
And, though despairing of relief,
In soft complaining vents his grief.

Then what should hinder but that I
Impatient of my wrongs may try
By saddest, softest strains to move
My wedded, latest, dearest love
To throw his cold neglect aside
And cheer once more his injured bride?

O thou whom sacred rites designed
My guide and husband ever kind,
My sovereign master, best of friends
On whom my earthly bliss depends,
If ever thou didst in Hetty see
Aught fair or good or dear to thee,
If gentle speech can ever move
The cold remains of former love,
Turn thee at last; my bosom ease;
Or tell my *why* I cease to please.

Is it because revolving years,
Heart-breaking sighs, and fruitless tears
Have quite deprived this form of mine
Of all that once thou fanciedst fine?
Ah, no! what once allured thy sight
Is still in its meridian height.

These eyes their usual lustre show
When uneclipsed by flowing woe:
Old age and wrinkles in this face
As yet could never find a place:
A youthful grace informs these lines
Where still the purple current shines
Unless, by thy ungentle art,
It flies to aid my wretched heart;
Nor does this slighted bosom show
The thousand hours it spends in woe.

    Or is it that, oppressed with care,
I stun with loud complaints thine ear
And make thy home, for quiet meant,
The seat of noise and discontent?
Ah, no! those ears were ever free
From matrimonial melody.
For though thine absence I lament
When half the lonely night is spent,
Yet, when the watch or early morn
Has brought me hopes of thy return,
I oft have wiped these watchful eyes,
Concealed my cares, and curbed my sighs
In spite of grief, to let thee see
I wore an endless smile for thee.

    Had I not practised every art
To oblige, divert, and cheer thy heart,
To make me pleasing in thine eyes
And turn thy house to paradise,

I had not asked, 'Why dost thou shun
These faithful arms and eager run
To some obscure, unclean retreat
With fiends incarnate glad to meet,
The vile companions of thy mirth,
The scum and refuse of the earth
Who, when inspired by beer, can grin
At witless oaths and jests obscene
Till the most learned of the throng
Begins a tale of ten hours long;
While thou, in raptures, with stretched jaws,
Crownest each joke with loud applause?'

 Deprived of freedom, health, and ease,
And rivalled by such *things* as these,
This latest effort will I try
Or to regain thy heart or die.
Soft as I am, I'll make thee see
I will not brook contempt from thee!

 Then quit the shuffling, doubtful sense,
Nor hold me longer in suspense,
Unkind, ungrateful as thou art,
Say—must I never regain thy heart?
Must all attempts to please thee prove
Unable to regain thy love?

 If so, by truth itself I swear,
The sad reverse I cannot bear.
No rest, no pleasure will I see—
My whole of bliss is lost with thee!

I'll give all thoughts of patience o'er
(A gift I never lost before),
Indulge at once my rage and grief,
Mourn obstinate, disdain relief,
And call that wretch my mortal foe
Who tries to mitigate my woe,
Till life, on terms severe as these,
Shall ebbing leave my heart at ease,
To thee thy liberty restore
To laugh, when Hetty is no more.

*Mehetabel Wright (1697-1750)*

# SOLITUDE

There is the loneliness of peopled places:
Streets roaring with their human flood; the crowd
That fills bright rooms with billowing sounds and faces,
Like foreign music, overshrill and loud.
There is the loneliness of one who stands
Fronting the waste under the cold sea-light,
A wisp of flesh against the endless sands,
Like a lost gull in solitary flight.
Single is all up-rising and down-lying;
Struggle or fear or silence none may share;
Each is alone in bearing and in dying;
Conquest is uncompanioned as despair.
Yet I have known no loneliness like this,
Locked in your arms and bent beneath your kiss.

*Babette Deutsch (b.1895)*

# WOMEN

women
lie open
as green meadows
to the urgent flood

compassion
for the erect member
and hand trembling

over shoulders
gazing
at different wallpapers
compassionate
and lonely
as the travelling moon

*Frances Horovitz (1938-83)*

# SONG

I love you, Mrs. Acorn. Would your husband mind
if I kissed you under the autumn sun,
if my brown-leaf guilty passion made you blind
to his manly charms and fun?

I want you, Mrs. Acorn. Do you think you'll come
to see my tangled, windswept desires,
and visit me in my everchanging house of some
vision of winter's fires?

I am serious Mrs. Acorn, do you hear?
Forget your family and other ties,
Come with me to where there is no fear,
where we'll find summer butterflies.

I am serious Mrs. Acorn, are you deaf?

*Kath Fraser (b.1947)*

## 'I AM BESET WITH A DREAM
## OF FAIR WOMAN'

I am beset with a dream of fair woman,
Lunatic for Venus flesh
So sweet in the night
I do not know if I have woven her,
Pygmalion, out of my desires
Or if indeed those hours she lay
Beside, under me.
Happy the hand that touches her,
The cloth that drapes her,
The eyes and words that catch hers.
Where she is the skies are
Clouded with loves, the minutes dove drawn.
I whimper in this waking sleep
Remembering as dogs run down past quarry,
Hunter and snared by my dreams of fair woman,
Lunatic for your Venus flesh.

*Maureen Duffy (b.1933)*

## OPPENHEIM'S CUP AND SAUCER

She asked me to luncheon in fur. Far from
the loud laughter of men, our secret life stirred.

I remember her eyes, the slim rope of her spine.
This is your cup, she whispered, and this mine.

We drank the sweet hot liquid and talked dirty.
As she undressed me, her breasts were a mirror

and there were mirrors in the bed. She said Place
your legs around my neck, that's right. Yes.

*Carol Ann Duffy (b.1955)*

# SECOND THOUGHTS

I thought of leaving her for a day
In town, it was such iron winter
At Durdans, the garden frosty clay,
The woods as dry as any splinter,
The sky congested. I would break
From the deep, lethargic, country air
To the shining lamps, to the clash of the play,
And to-morrow, wake
Beside her, a thousand things to say.
I planned—O more—I had almost started;—
I lifted her face in my hands to kiss,—
A face in a border of fox's fur,
For the bitter black wind had stricken her,
And she wore it—her soft hair straying out
Where it buttoned against the gray, leather snout:
In an instant we should have parted;
But at sight of the delicate world within
That fox-fur collar, from brow to chin,
At sight of those wonderful eyes from the mine,
Coal pupils, an iris of glittering spa,
And the wild, ironic, defiant shine
As of a creature behind a bar
One has captured, and, when three lives are past,
May hope to reach the heart of at last,
All that, and the love at her lips, combined
To shew me what folly it were to miss
A face with such thousand things to say,
And beside these, such thousand more to spare,
For the shining lamps, for the clash of the play—
O madness; not for a single day
Could I leave her! I stayed behind.

*Michael Field (1846-1914 & 1862-1913)*

## TO MY EXCELLENT LUCASIA, ON OUR FRIENDSHIP

I did not live until this time
   Crown'd my felicity,
When I could say without a crime,
   I am not thine, but Thee.

This carcass breath'd, and walkt, and slept,
   So that the World believ'd
There was a soul the motions kept;
   But they were all deceiv'd.

For as a watch by art is wound
   To motion, such was mine:
But never had Orinda found
   A soul till she found thine;

Which now inspires, cures, and supplies,
   And guides my darkened breast:
For thou art all that I can prize,
   My joy, my Life, my Rest.

No bridegroom's nor crown-conqueror's mirth
   To mine compared can be:
They have but pieces of the earth,
   I've all the World in thee.

Then let our flames still light and shine,
   And no false fear control,
As innocent as our design,
   Immortal as our soul.

*Katherine Philips  (1631-64)*

## MY MOUTH HOVERS ACROSS
## YOUR BREASTS

My mouth hovers across your breasts
in the short grey winter afternoon
in this bed   we are delicate
and touch   so hot with joy we amaze ourselves
tough   and delicate   we play rings
around each other   our daytime candle burns
with its peculiar light   and if the snow
begins to fall outside   filling the branches
and if the night falls   without announcement
these are the pleasures of winter
sudden, wild and delicate   your fingers
exact   my tongue exact at the same moment
stopping to laugh at a joke
my love   hot on your scent   on the cusp of winter

*Adrienne Rich (b.1929)*

# LOVE U.S.A.

love in the peaceful u.s.a.
draw the shades down
draw
our light limbs together

and let us love gently
as if
that's still possible

not heaving and struggling
like
in the movies

with bosomy gasps as
the man
takes her over

I'll tame you my
vixen as
he rips

off her clothes:
she sighs
aaaahhhhh.  Not

like young re-
volutionaries
shouting and fucking

sweating out power
more
power in bed

fighting the
system by
freeing your body

till you are a
cipher in
some weird class struggle.   No   love

me    lie down and
close out the country
and close out

tradition
and turn off the
tv

and let the newspapers
pile up on
the doorstep

and kick in the
radio    see how the
rhetoric dribbles away

and for once let's be
lyrical
like in the

poems
let's
pretend.


*Kathleen Spivack (b.1938)*

## From SILENT IS THE HOUSE

Come, the wind may never again
Blow as now it blows for us;
And the stars may never again shine as now they shine;
Long before October returns,
Seas of blood will have parted us;
And you must crush the love in your heart, and I the love
    in mine!

*Emily Brontë (1818-48)*

# SONNET FROM THE PORTUGUESE XLIII

Beloved, thou hast brought me many flowers
    Plucked in the garden, all the summer through
    And winter, and it seemed as if they grew
In this close room, nor missed the sun and showers,
So, in the like name of that love of ours,
    Take back these thoughts which here unfolded too,
    And which on warm and cold days I withdrew
From my heart's ground. Indeed, those beds and bowers
    Be overgrown with bitter weeds and rue,
And wait thy weeding; yet here's eglantine,
    Here's ivy!—take them, as I used to do
Thy flowers, and keep them where they shall not pine.
    Instruct thine eyes to keep their colours true,
And tell thy soul, their roots are left in mine.

*Elizabeth Barrett Browning  (1806-61)*

# PARABLE OF THE FOUR-POSTER

Because she wants to touch him,
she moves away.
Because she wants to talk to him,
she keeps silent.
Because she wants to kiss him,
she turns away
& kisses a man she does not want to kiss.

He watches
thinking she does not want him.
He listens
hearing her silence.
He turns away
thinking her distant
& kisses a girl he does not want to kiss.

They marry each other—
a four-way mistake.
He goes to bed with his wife
thinking of her.
She goes to bed with her husband
thinking of him.
—& all this in a real old-fashioned four-poster bed.

Do they live unhappily ever after?
Of course.
Do they undo their mistakes ever?
Never.
Who is the victim here?
Love is the victim.
Who is the villain?
Love that never dies.

*Erica Jong (b.1942)*

# WHEN I WAS FAIR AND YOUNG

When I was fair and young, then favour graced me;
Of many was I sought their mistress for to be,
But I did scorn them all, and answered them therefore:
'Go! go! go! seek some other where, importune me no more!'

How many weeping eyes, I made to pine with woe!
How many sighing hearts! I have no skill to show.
Yet I the prouder grew, and still this spake therefore:
'Go! go! go! seek some other where, importune me no more!'

Then spake fair Venus' son that proud victorious boy,
Saying: You dainty dame for that you be so coy?
I will so pluck your plumes that you shall say no more:
'Go! go! go! seek some other where, importune me no more!'

As soon as he had said, such change grew in my breast,
That neither night nor day, I could take any rest.
Then lo! I did repent that I had said before:
'Go! go! go! seek some other where, importune me no more.'

*Elizabeth I (1533-1603)*

# SONNET FROM THE PORTUGUESE V

I lift my heavy heart up solemnly,
As once Electra her sepulchral urn,
And, looking in thine eyes, I overturn
The ashes at thy feet. Behold and see
What a great heap of grief lay hid in me,
And how the red wild sparkles dimly burn
Through the ashen greyness. If thy foot in scorn
Could tread them out to darkness utterly,
It might be well perhaps. But if instead
Thou wait beside me for the wind to blow
The grey dust up, . . . those laurels on thine head,
O My beloved, will not shield thee so,
That none of all the fires shall scorch and shred
The hair beneath. Stand further off then! Go.

*Elizabeth Barrett Browning (1806-61)*

# DO NOT MAKE THINGS TOO EASY

Do not make things too easy.
There are rocks and abysses in the mind
As well as meadows.
There are things knotty and hard: intractable.
Do not talk to me of love and understanding.
I am sick of blandishments.
I want the rock to be met by a rock.
If I am vile, and behave hideously,
Do not tell me it was just a misunderstanding.


*Martha Baird (1921–81)*

## PARADOX

My brain burns with hate of you.
I am like a green field swept by scorching wind,
Everything withers.
There is nothing left of promise
But black death. Yet in my heart is our eternal love,
Hard and pure as a moonstone,
And like an opal,
Subtle with change.

*Anna Wickham (1884-1947)*

## IS/NOT

Love is not a profession
genteel or otherwise

sex is not dentistry
the slick filling of aches and cavities

you are not my doctor
you are not my cure,

nobody has that
power, you are merely a fellow/traveller

Give up this medical concern,
buttoned, attentive,

permit yourself anger
and permit me mine

which needs neither
your approval nor your surprise

which does not need to be made legal
which is not against a disease

but against you,
which does not need to be understood

or washed or cauterized,
which needs instead

to be said and said.
Permit me the present tense.


*Margaret Atwood (b.1939)*

# THE WINE IS DRUNK

The wine is drunk, the woman known.
Someone is generous darkness dries
unmanly tears for what's not found
in flesh, or anywhere. He lies
beside his love, and still alone.

Pride is a lie. His finger follows
eye, nostril, outline of the cheek.
Mortal fatigue has humbled his
exulting flesh, and all he'd seek
in a loved body's gulfs and hollows

changes to otherness: he'll never
ravish the secret of its grace.

I must be absent from myself,
must learn to praise love's waking face,
raise this unleavened heart, and sever

from my true life this ignorant sorrow.
I must in this gross darkness cherish
more than all plenitude the hunger
that drives the spirit. Flesh must perish
yet still, tomorrow and tomorrow

be faithful to the last, an old
blind dog that knows the stairs, and stays
obedient as it climbs and suffers.
My love, the light we'll wake to praise
beats darkness to a dust of gold.

*Gwen Harwood (b.1920)*

# ACCOUTREMENT

But lovers are like umbrellas arnt they?
They're like gloves
They cover you up, they keep you warm
They look so good, they fit so nice
they shield you.
Then you leave them on a train
You think 'How did I manage *that?*'
    And   'I didn't like them anyway.'
    Or    'I've lost them.'


*'Marnia'* (1968–92)

# THE FEATHER

A man and woman walking
Up the rye hill
Had no breath for talking.
The evening was still;

Only the wind in the rough grass
Made a papery patter;
Like yesterday it was,
Too spent a sigh to matter.

Down fell a curlew's feather
As they went on their way
(Who walked kindly together
And had nothing to say),

So light, so soft, so strange,
To have settled on her heart.
It was the breath of change,
That breathed them apart.

*Lilian Bowes Lyon (1895-1949)*

## SEA LOVE

Tide be runnin' the great world over:
    'Twas only last June month I mind that we
Was thinkin' the toss and the call in the breast of the lover
    So everlastin' as the sea.

Heer's the same little fishes that sputter and swim,
    Wi' the moon's old glim on the grey, wet sand;
An' him no more to me nor me to him
    Than the wind goin' over my hand.

*Charlotte Mew (1869-1928)*

# THE FALL

For some years he still would harden as he
Pushed his fingers through my stubbly hair,
Then gathering my small breasts in his fists
Would bite them, murmuring of a glorious fruit
He'd tasted once in Singapore.
    At twenty
He'd impressed me with his rooms large enough
To run in, with his nonchalance for glass,
With the books he'd hold but never open.
There was the gift of his cool hands along
My shoulder blades, of the olives he'd split
And stone: pressing their charcoal flesh against
My tongue, *These taste of you*, he whispered, once.
In his absence I'd wait all day in the orchard
Longing for his fruit to fall. Still innocent
And pre-Newtonian I'd lie beneath the *Worcester*
*Pearmain* watching the sour fruits soften to rot.
He'd spend entire weekends training his beloved
Nectarines and damsons, cherries, apricots
And pears—the reluctant he'd hard-prune back,
Or whip-graft their rootstocks.
    The day I left
I watched him nail his favoured espalier apple,
Arm by arm, against a reddened wall.

*Sarah Maguire (b.1957)*

# DEAD LOVE

Oh never weep for love that's dead
Since love is seldom true
But changes his fashion from blue to red,
From brightest red to blue,
And love was born to an early death
And is so seldom true.

Then harbour no smile on your bonny face
To win the deepest sigh.
The fairest words on truest lips
Pass on and surely die,
And you will stand alone, my dear,
When wintry winds draw nigh.

Sweet, never weep for what cannot be,
For this God has not given.
If the merest dream of love were true
Then, sweet, we should be in heaven,
And this is only earth, my dear,
Where true love is not given.

*Elizabeth Siddal (1834-62)*

## LOVE AND FRIENDSHIP

Love is like the wild rose-briar,
Friendship like the holly-tree—
The holly is dark when the rose-briar blooms
But which will bloom most constantly?

The wild rose-briar is sweet in spring,
Its summer blossoms scent the air;
Yet wait till winter comes again
And who will call the wild-briar fair?

Then scorn the silly rose-wreath now
And deck thee with the holly's sheen,
That when December blights thy brow
He still may leave thy garland green.


*Emily Brontë (1818-48)*

# HAPPY ENDING

After they had not made love
she pulled the sheet up over her eyes
until he was buttoning his shirt:
not shyness for their bodies—those
they had willingly displayed—but a frail
endeavour to apologise.

Later, though, drawn together by
a distaste for such 'untidy ends'
they agreed to meet again; whereupon
they giggled, reminisced, held hands
as though what they had made was love—
and not that happier outcome, friends.


*Fleur Adcock (b.1934)*

# THE HARES

i
Immobile, but fearless,
　　With peace in her eyes,
The shy hare of friendship
　　Scarce a yard from him lies.

He has stretched a swift hand
　　To caress the free head.
The shy hare that was friendship
　　To the covert has sped.

ii
The wild hare of love
　　Is alert at his feet.
Oh, the fierce quivering heart!
　　Oh, the heart's fierce beat!

He has tightened his noose.
　　It was fine as a thread;
But the wild hare that was love
　　At his feet lies dead.


*Susan Miles (late 19th/early 20th century)*

# WE WHO HAVE LOVED

We who have loved, alas! may not be friends,
Too faint, or yet too fierce the stifled fire,—
A random spark—and lo! our dread desire
Leaps into flame, as though to make amends
For chill, blank days, and with strange fury rends
The dying embers of Love's funeral pyre.
Electric, charged anew, the living wire
A burning message through our torpor sends.
Could we but pledge with loyal hearts and eyes
A friendship worthy of the fair, full past,
Now mutilate, and lost beyond recall,
Then might a Phoenix from its ashes rise
Fit for a soul flight; but we find, aghast,
Love must be nothing if not all in all.

*Corinne Roosevelt Robinson (late 19th/early 20th century)*

# ENCOUNTER

We meet again.
You are as brief, staccato in your wonder as a leaf in autumn:
"It is a joy! . . . It has been so long!" . . .
As leaves—yellow, red, or brown—your words flutter down.
There is nothing to say, anyway.
You are you.
I can rub my hand against your coat—
It will be rough and my nails will catch upon the threads,
And your head will be held high, your lips will smile
For each passer-by.

You are no mystery to me:
I have grown wise with thinking on your beauty;
I could let your beauty slip like grains of sand
Between my fingers, and could find each grain again
And hold it in the hollow of my hand.

The sun lengthens our shadows into one;
We move along.
The sound of our feet against the stone pavement,
Swift and hard;
The sound of our feet descending a stair;
Warm air fawning about us,
Laughter that bursts like a red balloon, as soon forgotten.
Laughter, warm air, small painted chairs, a table,
    yellow cups, tea -
My thoughts lie like dust upon the bloom of the room.

We are together;
There is still the singing truth of our youth;
We may go as a feather goes beyond the wind that blows it.
"The days have been so very long away from you" -
You light a cigarette -
"So very long!" The smoke curls a ring around your suffering.

Ah well, your lies are as a warmth of sun pressing the lids
    over my eyes,
And I am tired.

I would remember summer: hours that fell as fruit upon the
    ground,
As fruit were held, tasted, thrown away;
Each day opening its petals to another day.
Summer! Tendrils of heat drawing us down—
Sweet, sweet earth!
Rain lisping to flowers . . .

"Do you still take three lumps in your tea?"—you smile,
Lean forward as you speak; shadows shift:
Your hair is smooth as lacquer, light glides upon it—
And still get perfume from Piver?"
I feel the color in my cheek.

What does it matter anyway?
The breath of winter blurs the window-pane—
And if we love again, what does it matter?
I would remember summer:
There is still the harvest moon—soon it will be over,
Very soon.

You rise, you are sorry, you must go—
"It was a joy! . . . It has been so long!"
We reach the street.

And I am swayed as a blade of grass beneath the wind.
As the wind you are gone.

*Marion Strobel (fl.1920s)*

# WHEN LAST WE PARTED

When last we parted, thou wert young and fair,
    How beautiful let fond remembrance say!
    Alas! since then old time has stolen away
Full thirty years, leaving my temples bare.—
So has it perished like a thing of air,
    The dream of love and youth!—now both are grey
    Yet still remembering that delightful day,
Though time with his cold touch has blanched my hair,
    Though I have suffered many years of pain
Since then, though I did never think to live
    To hear that voice or see those eyes again,
I can a sad but cordial greeting give,
And for thy welfare breathe as warm a prayer—
As when I loved thee young and fair.

*Catherine Maria Fanshawe (1765-1834)*

## IN RECOMPENSE

Now for the long years when I could not love you,
I bring in recompense this gift of yearning—
A luminous vase uplifted to the sun,
Blue with the shadows of near-twilight.
Here in its full round symmetry of darkness,
Burning with swift curved flashes bright as tears,
I lift it to the lonely lips that knew
Its slow creation, and the wheel of sorrow turning.
Take it with hands like faded petals,
White as the moonlight of our garden;
And for the long years when I could not love you
Drink from its amber-colored night.


*Eda Lou Walton (fl.1920s)*

# THE FLIGHT

Look back with longing eyes and know that I will follow,
Lift me up in your love as a light wing lifts a swallow,
Let our flight be far in sun or blowing rain—
*But what if I heard my first love calling me again?*

Hold me on your heart as the brave sea holds the foam,
Take me far away to the hills that hide your home:
Peace shall thatch the roof and love shall latch the door—
*But what if I heard my first love calling me once more?*


*Sara Teasdale (1884-1933)*

## AT LES DEUX MAGOTS

The bloom on the fruit is perfect.
His moist eyes are fixed on her.
As he hands her plums she thinks
he is the kind of man who'd kiss her
on the lips in friendship,
to whom she'd try to turn a cheek in time.
*The way he gives me ripeness*
*when what I want is something raw.*

An old memory makes the blood
rock in her veins: a glimpse of Ford
in the street, his face turned from her,
his arms full of books,
that moment polished like a piece of bone.
Her thoughts are all crooked now,
her hands cold in their thin cotton gloves,
she takes the plums from him dumbly.

*Maura Dooley (b.1957)*

# WORTH DYING FOR

If we shall live, we live:
    If we shall die; we die:
If we live we shall meet again:
    But to-night, good-bye.
One word, let but one be heard—
    What, not one word?

If we sleep we shall wake again
    And see to-morrow's light:
If we wake, we shall meet again:
    But to-night, good-night.
Good-night, my lost and found—
    Still not a sound?

    If we live, we must part;
If we die, we part in pain:
    If we die, we shall part
    Only to meet again.
By those tears on either cheek,
    To-morrow you will speak.

    To meet, worth living for:
    Worth dying for, to meet,
    To meet, worth parting for:
    Bitter forgot in sweet.
    To meet, worth parting before,
    Never to part more.

*Christina Rossetti (1830-94)*

# 'TIS CUSTOMARY AS WE PART

'Tis customary as we part
A trinket—to confer—
It helps to stimulate the faith
When lovers be afar—

'Tis various—as the various taste—
Clematis—journeying for—
Presents me with a single Curl
Of her Electric Hair—

*Emily Dickinson (1830-86)*

IN THE ORCHARD

"I thought you loved me." "No, it was only
    fun."
"When we stood there, closer than all?" "Well,
    the harvest moon
"Was shining and queer in your hair, and it
    turned my head."
"That made you?" "Yes." "Just the moon
    and the light it made
"Under the tree?" "Well, your mouth, too."
    "Yes, my mouth?"
"And the quiet there that sang like the drum in
    the booth.
"You shouldn't have danced like that." "Like
    what?" "So close,
"With your head turned up, and the flower in
    your hair, a rose
"That smelt all warm." "I loved you. I thought
    you knew
"I wouldn't have danced like that with any but
    you."
I didn't know. I thought you knew it was fun."
"I thought it was love you meant." "Well, it's
    done." "Yes, it's done.
"I've seen boys stone a blackbird, and watched
    them drown
"A kitten . . . it clawed at the reeds, and they
    pushed it down
"Into the pool while it screamed. Is that fun,
    too?"
"Well, boys are like that . . . Your brothers . . ."
    "Yes, I know.
"But you, so lovely and strong! Not you! Not
    you!"
"They don't understand it's cruel. It's only a
    game."

"And are girls fun, too?"  "No, still in a way
    it's the same.
"It's queer and lovely to have a girl . . ."  "Go
    on."
"It makes you mad for a bit to feel she's your
    own,
"And you laugh and kiss her, and maybe you
    give her a ring,
"But it's only in fun."  "But I gave you every-
    thing."
"Well, you shouldn't have done it. You know
    what a fellow thinks
"When a girl does that."  "Yes, he talks of her
    over his drinks
"And calls her a—"  "Stop that now. I thought
    you knew."
"But it wasn't with anyone else. It was only
    you."
"How did I know? I thought you wanted it too.
"I thought you were like the rest. Well, what's
    to be done?"
"To be done?"  "Is it all right?"  "Yes."
    "Sure?"  "Yes, but why?"
"I don't know. I thought you were going to cry.
"You said you had something to tell me."  "Yes,
    I know.
"It wasn't anything really . . . I think I'll go."
"Yes, it's late. There's thunder about, a drop
    of rain
"Fell on my hand in the dark. I'll see you again
"At the dance next week. You're sure that every-
    thing's right?"
"Yes."  "Well, I'll be going."  "Kiss me . . ."
    "Good night." . . . "Good night."

*Muriel Stuart (d.1967)*

# TO COLINDRA

*Love* without *Hope* is like *Breath* without *Air*,
An impossible *Joy*, a ridiculous *Care*;
Yet *Cupid*, like *Alchimy* runs us a-ground,
In quest of *Projection* which never was found:
And tho' *numberless Ruins* around you may view,
Yet so pleasing 's the Madness, *their Steps you pursue.*

*Elizabeth Thomas (1675-1731)*

# APPEAL

Daphnis dearest, wherefore weave me
Webs of lies lest truth should grieve me?
I could pardon much, believe me:
Dower me, Daphnis, or bereave me,
Kiss me, kill me, love me, leave me,—
Damn me, dear, but don't deceive me!

*Edith Nesbit (1858-1924)*

# INFELICE

Walking swiftly with a dreadful duchess,
He smiled too briefly, his face was as pale as sand,
He jumped into a taxi when he saw me coming,
Leaving me alone with a private meaning,
He loves me so much, my heart is singing.
Later at the Club when I rang him in the evening
They said: Sir Rat is dining, is dining, is dining,
No Madam, he left no message, ah how his silence speaks,
He loves me too much for words, my heart is singing.
The Pullman seats are here, the tickets for Paris, I am waiting,
Presently the telephone rings, it is his valet speaking,
Sir Rat is called away, to Scotland, his constituents,
(Ah the dreadful duchess, but he loves me best)
Best pleasure to the last, my heart is singing.
One night he came, it was four in the morning,
Walking slowly upstairs, he stands beside my bed,
Dear darling, lie beside me, it is too cold to stand speaking,
He lies down beside me, his face is like the sand,
He is in a sleep of love, my heart is singing.
Sleeping softly softly, in the morning I must wake him,
And waking he murmurs, I only came to sleep.
The words are so sweetly cruel, how deeply he loves me,
I say them to myself alone, my heart is singing.
Now the sunshine strengthens, it is ten in the morning,
He is so timid in love, he only needs to know,
He is my little child, how can he come if I do not call him,
I will write and tell him everything, I take the pen and write:
I love you so much, my heart is singing.

*Stevie Smith (1902-71)*

# SONG

How hardly I concealed my tears,
    How oft did I complain!
When, many tedious days, my fears
    Told me I loved in vain.

But now my joys as wild are grown,
    And hard to be concealed;
Sorrow may make a silent moan,
    But joy will be revealed.

I tell it to the bleating flocks,
    To every stream and tree;
And bless the hollow murmuring rocks
    For echoing back to me.

Thus you may see with how much joy
    We want, we wish, believe;
'Tis hard such passion to destroy
    But easy to deceive.

*Anne Wharton (?1659-85)*

# THE WAY OF IT

This is the way of it, wide world over,
One is beloved, and one is the lover,
     One gives and the other receives.
One lavishes all in a wild emotion,
One offers a smile for a life's devotion,
     One hopes and the other believes,
One lies awake in the night to weep,
And the other drifts off in a sweet sound sleep.

One soul is aflame with a godlike passion,
One plays with love in an idler's fashion,
     One speaks and the other hears.
One sobs, 'I love you,' and wet eyes show it,
And one laughs lightly, and says, 'I know it,'
     With smiles for the other's tears.
One lives for the other and nothing beside,
And the other remembers the world is wide.

This is the way of it, sad earth over,
The heart that breaks is the heart of the lover,
     And the other learns to forget.
'For what is the use of endless sorrow?
Though the sun goes down, it will rise to-morrow;
     And life is not over yet.'
Oh! I know this truth, if I know no other,
That passionate Love is Pain's own mother.

*Ella Wheeler Wilcox (1850–1919)*

# SONG OF THE FUCKED DUCK

In using there are always two.
The manipulator dances with a partner who cons herself.
There are lies that glow so brightly we consent
to give a finger and then an arm
to let them burn.
I was dazzled by the crowd where everyone called my name.
Now I stand outside the funhouse exit, down the slide
reading my guidebook of Marx in Esperanto
and if I don't know anymore which way means forward
down is where my head is, next to my feet
with a pocketful of words and plastic tokens.


*Marge Piercy (b.1936)*

# TIDES

O patient shore, that canst not go to meet
Thy love, the restless sea, how comfortest
Thou all thy loneliness? Art thou at rest,
When, loosing his strong arms from round thy feet,
He turns away? Know'st thou, however sweet
That other shore may be, that to thy breast
He must return? And when in sterner test
He folds thee to a heart which does not beat,
Wraps thee in ice, and gives no smile, no kiss,
To break long wintry days, still dost thou miss
Naught from thy trust? Still wait, unfaltering,
The higher, warmer waves which leap in spring?
O sweet, wise shore, to be so satisfied!
O heart, learn from the shore! Love has a tide!

*Helen Hunt Jackson (1830-85)*

## From FELIX HOLT, THE RADICAL

Why, there are maidens of heroic touch
And yet they seem like things of gossamer
You'd pinch the life out of, as out of moths.
O, it is not fond tones and mouthingness,
'Tis not the arms akimbo and large strides,
That makes a woman's force. The tiniest birds,
With softest downy breasts, have passions in them,
And are brave with love.

*George Eliot (1819-80)*

# ON THE THRESHOLD

O god, my dream! I dreamed that you were dead;
Your mother hung above the couch and wept
Whereon you lay all white, and garlanded
With blooms of waxen whiteness. I had crept
Up to your chamber-door, which stood ajar,
And in the doorway watched you from afar,
Nor dared advance to kiss your lips and brow.
I had no part nor lot in you, as now;
Death had not broken between us the old bar;
Nor torn from out my heart the old, cold sense
Of your misprision and my impotence.

*Amy Levy (1861-89)*

# THE BUNGLER

You glow in my heart
Like the flames of uncounted candles.
But when I go to warm my hands,
My clumsiness overturns the light,
And then I stumble
Against the tables and chairs.

*Amy Lowell (1874-1925)*

# THE STORM

Down poured the rain; the closed window streamed
With its cold tears; leaden hung the leaves
With a load of rain, heavier than grief,
And the white trumpets of bindweed flowers, the open
Trumpets of joy and summer were splashed with rain,
Stained like the faces of children scattered with tears.
There was no word, you rose and walked away,
And all I saw were the pale heart-shaped leaves
Of bindweed clinging above their ruined flowers,
And the rain falling, more silently than tears.

*Margaret Stanley-Wrench (b.1916)*

## I WANT TO LOVE YOU
## VERY MUCH


I want to love you very much

You ask for my love
    I am afraid to give what I have
A gentle animal leans on my arm
    I hurt you
You look at me with wounded eyes
    I slap you
You beg for my love
    I leave you.


*'Marnia' (1968-92)*

# THE MEETING

We started speaking,
Looked at each other, then turned away.
The tears kept rising to my eyes.
But I could not weep.
I wanted to take your hand
But my hand trembled.
You kept counting the days
Before we should meet again.
But both of us felt in our hearts
That we parted for ever and ever.
The ticking of the little clock filled the quiet room.
"Listen," I said. "It is so loud,
Like a horse galloping on a lonely road,
As loud as a horse galloping past in the night."
You shut me up in your arms.
But the sound of the clock stifled our hearts' beating.
You said, "I cannot go: all that is living of me
Is here for ever and ever."
Then you went.
The world changed. The sound of the clock grew fainter,
Dwindled away, became a minute thing.
I whispered in the darkness, "If it stops, I shall die."

*Katherine Mansfield (1888-1923)*

# THE TAXI

When I go away from you
The world beats dead
Like a slackened drum.
I call out for you against the jutted stars
And shout into the ridges of the wind.
Streets coming fast,
One after the other,
Wedge you away from me,
And the lamps of the city prick my eyes
So that I can no longer see your face.
Why should I leave you,
To wound myself upon the sharp edges of the night?

*Amy Lowell (1874-1925)*

## A LETTER TO HER HUSBAND, ABSENT UPON PUBLICK EMPLOYMENT

As loving Hind that (Hartless) wants her Deer,
Scuds through the woods and fern with harkning ear,
Perplext, in every bush and nook doth pry
Her dearest Deer might answer ear or eye:
So doth my anxious soul, which now doth miss
A dearer Dear (far dearer Heart) than this,
Still wait with doubts, and hopes, and failing eye,
His voice to hear or person to discry.
Or as the pensive Dove doth all alone
On withered bough most uncouthly bemoan
The absence of her Love and loving Mate,
Whose loss hath made her so unfortunate:
Ev'n thus doe I, with many a deep sad groan,
Bewail my turtle true, who now is gone,
His presence and his safe return still woo
With thousand dolefull sighs and mournfull Coo.
Or as the loving Mullet, that true Fish
Her fellow lost, nor joy nor life doth wish,
But lanches on that shore, there for to dye
Where she her captive husband doth espy.
Mine being gone, I lead a joyless life,
I have a loving fere, yet seem no wife:
But worst of all, to him can't steer my course,
I here, he there, alas, both kept by force.
Return my Dear, my joy, my only Love,
Unto thy Hinde, thy Mullet and thy Dove,
Who neither joyes in pasture, house nor streams:
The substance gone, O me, these are but dreams.
Together at one Tree, oh let us brouze,
And like two Turtles roost within one house,
And like the Mullets in one River glide,
Let's still remain but one, till death divide.
    Thy loving Love and Dearest Dear,
      At home, abroad, and everywhere.

*Anne Bradstreet (?1613-72)*

226

# MY LIFE CLOSED TWICE

My life closed twice before its close;
    It yet remains to see
If Immortality unveil
    A third event to me,

So huge, so hopeless to conceive,
    As these that twice befell.
Parting is all we know of heaven,
    And all we need of hell.


*Emily Dickinson (1830-86)*

# GIFTS

You ask me what since we must part
You shall bring back to me.
Bring back a pure and faithful heart
As true as mine to thee.

You talk of gems from foreign lands,
Of treasure, spoil, and prize.
Ah love! I shall not search your hands
But look into your eyes.

*Juliana Horatia Ewing (1841-85)*

# AT PARTING

Since we through war awhile must part
Sweetheart, and learn to lose
Daily use
Of all that satisfied our heart:
Lay up those secrets and those powers
Wherewith you pleased and cherished me these two years:

Now we must draw, as plants would,
On tubers stored in a better season,
Our honey and heaven;
Only our love can store such food.
Is this to make a god of absence?
A new-born monster to steal our sustenance?

We cannot quite cast out lack and pain.
Let him remain—what he may devour
We can well spare:
He never can tap this, the true vein.
I have no words to tell you what you were,
But when you are sad, think, Heaven could give no more.

*Anne Ridler (b.1912)*

## From CHLOE AND MYRA

Blindfold I should to Myra run,
And swear to love her ever;
Yet when the bandage was undone,
Should only think her clever.

With the full usage of my eyes,
I Chloe should decide for;
But when she talks, I her despise,
Whom, dumb, I could have died for!

*Sophia Burrell (?1750-1802)*

# SONNET FROM THE PORTUGUESE XIV

If thou must love me, let it be for nought
Except for love's sake only. Do not say
"I love her for her smile . . her look . . her way
Of speaking gently, . . for a trick of thought
That falls in well with mine, and certes brought
A sense of pleasant ease on such a day"—
For these things in themselves, Beloved, may
Be changed, or change for thee,—and love so wrought,
May be unwrought so. Neither love me for
Thine own dear pity's wiping my cheeks dry,
Since one might well forget to weep who bore
Thy comfort long, and lose thy love thereby.
But love me for love's sake, that evermore
Thou may'st love on through love's eternity.

*Elizabeth Barrett Browning (1806-61)*

# A LETTER TO DAPHNIS

This to the crown and blessing of my life,
The much loved husband of a happy wife;
To him whose constant passion found the art
To win a stubborn and ungrateful heart,
And to the world by tenderest proof discovers
They err, who say that husbands can't be lovers.
With such return of passion as is due,
Daphnis I love, Daphnis my thoughts pursue;
Daphnis my hopes and joys are bounded all in you.
Even I, for Daphnis' and my promise' sake,
What I in women censure, undertake.
But this from love, not vanity, proceeds;
You know who writes, and I who 'tis that reads.
Judge not my passion by my want of skill:
Many love well, though they express it ill;
And I your censure could with pleasure bear,
Would you but soon return, and speak it here.

*Ann Finch (1661-1720)*

## 'MY TRUE LOVE HATH MY HEART'

How can I write about you
When you are all the world?
When I know
That all that is good or just in me is only
An echo of you:
When all that I think is what you have breathed on my heart:
And all I say,
Although I am praised for it,
Is your book read aloud.

*Naomi Mitchison (b.1897)*

# THREAD

If I love you
Your life instantly becomes
More fragile than my own,
Your body more frail
Each cough or minor pain
A symptom of some dread
Disease or other.

Death is on every road
Or in every other car
Some nights in my skin
Flutters in apprehension
And I am so threatened that
Caring translates itself
Inside my head to
Stone cold anger.

Because I am unsufficient
Tormented by the frailty
Of you whom I love.
Selfish I
Find you
Necessary for my own definition
Your life is a single thread
It snaps
I wither.

*Catherine Lucy Czerkawska (b.1950)*

# SYMPATHY

His pains so racked my heart
    That soon I had forgot
Whether in him or me they had their start.
    And though I had no lot
    In griefs that him abused
    I thought one day, confused,
If I should cease to feel, O God what gain!
    An end to all his pain.

*Viola Meynell (1888-1956)*

## VERSES WRITTEN ON HER DEATH-BED
## AT BATH TO HER HUSBAND IN LONDON

Thou who dost all my worldly thoughts employ,
Thou pleasing source of all my earthly joy,
Thou tenderest husband and thou dearest friend,
To thee this first, this last adieu I send!
At length the conqueror Death asserts his right,
And will for ever veil me from thy sight;
He woos me to him with a cheerful grace,
And not one terror clouds his meagre face;
He promises a lasting rest from pain,
And shows that all life's fleeting joys are vain;
Th' eternal scenes of Heaven he sets in view;
And tells me that no other joys are true.
But love, fond love, would yet resist his power,
Would fain awhile defer the parting hour;
He brings thy mourning image to my eyes,
And would obstruct my journey to the skies.
But say, thou dearest, thou unwearied friend!
Say, shouldst thou grieve to see my sorrows end?
Thou know'st a painful pilgrimage I've pass'd;
And shouldst thou grieve that rest is come at last?
Rather rejoice to see me shake off life,
And die as I have liv'd, thy faithful wife.

*Mary Monk (?1677-1715)*

# MY DEAREST DUST

My dearest dust, could not thy hasty day
Afford thy drowzy patience leave to stay
One hower longer: so that we might either
Sate up, or gone to bedd together?
But since thy finisht labor hath possest
Thy weary limbs with early rest,
Enjoy it sweetly: and thy widdowe bride
Shall soone repose her by thy slumbring side.
Whose business, now, is only to prepare
My nightly dress, and call to prayre:
Mine eyes wax heavy and ye day growes old.
The dew falls thick, my beloved growes cold.
Draw, draw ye closed curtaynes: and make room:
My dear, my dearest dust; I come, I come.

*Epitaph on monument erected in 1641 by Lady Catherine Dyer
to her husband Sir William Dyer in Colmworth Church, Bedfordshire*

## ETTRICK

When we first rade down Ettrick,
Our bridles were ringing, our hearts were dancing,
The waters were singing, the sun was glancing,
An' blithely our hearts rang out thegither,
As we brushed the dew frae the blooming heather,
    When we first rade down Ettrick.

When we next rade down Ettrick,
The day was dying, the wild birds calling,
The wind was sighing, the leaves were falling,
An' silent an' weary, but close thegither,
We urged our steeds thro' the faded heather,
    When we next rade down Ettrick.

When I last rade down Ettrick,
The winds were shifting, the storm was waking,
The snow was drifting, my heart was breaking,
For we never again were to ride thegither,
In sun or storm on the mountain heather,
    When I last rade down Ettrick.

*Lady John Scott (1810-1900)*

# AULD ROBIN FORBES

And auld Robin Forbes hes gien tem a dance,
I pat on my speckets to see them aw prance;
I thout o'the days when I was but fifteen,
And skipp'd wi' the best upon Forbes's green.
Of aw things that is I think thout is meast queer,
It brings that that's by-past  and sets it down here;
I see Willy as plain as I dui this bit leace,
When he tuik his cwoat lappet and deeghted his feace.

The lasses aw wonder'd what Willy cud see
In yen that was dark and hard featur'd leyke me;
And they wonder'd ay mair when they talk'd o' my wit,
And slily telt Willy that cudn't be it:
But Willy he laugh'd, and he meade me his weyfe,
And whea was mair happy thro' aw his lang leyfe?
It's e'en my great comfort, now Willy is geane,
That he offen said—nea place was leyke his awn heame!

I mind when I carried my wark to yon steyle
Where Willy was deykin, the time to beguile,
He wad fling me a daisy to put i' my breast,
And I hammer'd my noddle to mek out a jest.
But merry or grave, Willy often wad tell
There was nin o' the leave that was leyke my awn sel;
And he spak what he thout, for I'd hardly a plack
When we married, and nobbet ae gown to my back.

When the clock had struck eight I expected him heame,
And wheyles went to meet him as far as Dumleane;
Of aw hours it telt *eight* was dearest to me,
But now when it streykes there's a tear i' my ee.
O Willy! dear Willy! it never can be
That age, time, or death, can divide thee and me!
For that spot on earth that's aye dearest to me,
Is the turf that has cover'd my Willy frae me!

*Susanna Blamire (1747-94)*

# FREDDY

Nobody knows what I feel about Freddy
I cannot make anyone understand
I love him sub specie aeternitatis
I love him out of hand.
I don't love him so much in the restaurants that's a fact
To get him hobnob with my old pub chums needs too much tact
He don't love them and they don't love him
In the pub lub lights they say Freddy very dim.
But get him alone on the open saltings
Where the sea licks up to the fen
He is his and my own heart's best
World without end ahem.
People who say we ought to get married ought to get
     smacked:
Why should we do it when we can't afford it and have
     ourselves whacked?
Thank you kind friends and relations thank you,
We do very well as we do.
Oh what do I care for the pub lub lights
And the friends I love so well—
There's more in the way I feel about Freddy
Than a friend can tell.
But all the same I don't care much for his meelyoo I mean
I don't anheimate mich in the ha-ha well-off surburban scene
Where men are few and hearts go tumptytum
In the tennis club lub lights poet very dumb.
But there never was a boy like Freddy
For a haystack's ivory tower of bliss
Where speaking sub specie humanitatis
Freddy and me can kiss.
Exiled from his meelyoo
Exiled from mine
There's all Tom Tiddler's time pocket
For his love and mine.

*Stevie Smith (1902-71)*

## SOUS-ENTENDU

Don't think

that I don't know
that as you talk to me
the hand of your mind
is inconspicuously
taking off my stocking,
moving in resourceful blindness
up along my thigh.

Don't think
that I don't know
that you know
everything I say
is a garment.

*Anne Stevenson (b.1933)*

## TO ONE PERSUADING A LADY
## TO MARRIAGE

Forbear, bold Youth; all's Heaven here,
    And what you do aver,
To others courtship may appear,
    'Tis sacrilege to her.

She is a public deity;
    And were't not very odd
She should dispose herself to be
    A petty household god?

First make the Sun in private shine
    And bid the World adieu,
That so he may his beams confine
    In compliment to you:

But if of that you do despair,
    Think how you did amiss
To strive to fix her beams which are
    More bright and large than this.

*Katherine Philips (1631-64)*

# SEMI-SKILLED LOVER

Nothing like her ever came his way before
so he is a bit off his head. He welds
'I love you' under the bonnet of her car.
It is a passion so sharp it almost gelds

him. She doesn't know whether to laugh or cry.
Her children mock his boots wiped on her door mat.
Everything she has now fits, goes. His try
is to smooth her path, have all her needs off pat.

Yet he can never come at her, must fear to be
always the eager mongrel tolerated for
its willingness to please. Lopsided he
may clown to ingratiate, not be shown the door

dreading always the shadow over her threshold
of some smart talking *Times* turner, A or B.

*Maureen Duffy (b.1933)*

From CLIO

We every Day grew dearer to each other. I was then
indeed as blind as he. I gave him every Perfection, and
began to love in earnest. How did I want a Friend to
guard me from this Precipice, where Love was leading
me, to warn me of this Serpent, who was sacking out the
Sweetness of my Soul, and laying every Art to destroy it!

Honour, that Guardian Angel, can alone
Give Life to Love, and fix him on his Throne:
Or if from Beauty Passion ever springs,
How short its Reign, how ready are its Wings!
Or if from Wit the trifling Flame is born,
Soon it expires, and grows our Reason's Scorn.
'Tis artless Tenderness, and Honour join'd,
Can only triumph o'er a noble Mind.
With these *Hillarius* leads my Soul along,
How soft the gentle Chain, and yet, O God, how strong!

If all Mankind were plac'd before my Eyes,
The present, past, and all that shall hereafter rise,
With noble Scorn I'd look whole Nations o'er,
And only fix on him I now adore.
All that is charming in his Face appears,
Sweet Wisdom in the Bloom of sprightly Years.
For Adoration every Feature made,
Oh! how they charm! oh! God, how they persuade.
With awful Wonder I approach their Charms
With bending, trembling Knees, and longing Arms,
With Extacies that ne'er can be express'd,
But by my dying Eyes, where my fond Soul's confess'd.

*Martha Sansom (1690-1736)*

# ANGELLICA'S LAMENT

Had I remained in innocent security,
I should have thought all men were born my slaves,
And worn my power like lightning in my eyes,
To have destroyed at pleasure when offended.
—But when love held the mirror, the undeceiving glass
Reflected all the weakness of my soul, and made me know
My richest treasure being lost, my honour,
All the remaining spoil could not be worth
The conqueror's care or value.
—Oh how I fell like a long worshipped idol
Discovering all the cheat.


*Aphra Behn (1640-89)*

# VICIOUS CIRCLE

He nice frum far, but far frum nice,
He hips dus move like snake.
He make she HOT! Then numb-like ice,
(It more than she could take!)

He born to lie, she born to hear,
He really tell dem sweet!
An if real life try come too near,
She fast go make it fleet.

De bitter blow come quite a shock,
Experience really burned,
The fact he human, weak an bad,
Is hard lesson to learn.

Like soucouyant*, he suck she pride,      *vampire
An leave a harden shell,
So, when a really nice man come,
She *sure* to give him hell!

*Marsha Prescod*

# THE CAUTION

Soft kisses may be innocent;
But ah! too easy maid, beware;
Tho' that is all thy kindness meant,
'Tis love's delusive, fatal snare.

No virgin e'er at first design'd
Thro' all the maze of love to stray;
But each new path allures her mind,
Till wandering on, she lose her way.

'Tis easy ere set out to stay;
But who the useful art can teach,
When sliding down a steepy way,
To stop, before the end we reach?

Keep ever something in thy power,
Beyond what would thy honour stain:
He will not dare to aim at more,
Who for small favours sighs in vain.

*Catherine Cockburn (1679-1749)*

# LOVE ARM'D

Love in fantastic triumph sate,
    Whilst bleeding hearts around him flow'd,
For whom fresh pains he did create,
    And strange tyrannic power he shew'd.
From thy bright eyes he took his fires
    Which round about in sport he hurl'd,
But t'was from mine he took desires,
    Enough t'undo the amorous world.

From me he took his sighs and tears,
    From thee his pride and cruelty:
From me his languishments and fears,
    And ev'ry killing dart from thee.
Thus thou and I the god have arm'd,
    And set him up a deity:
But my poor heart alone is harm'd,
    While thine the victor is and free.

*Aphra Behn (1640-89)*

# SONG

Ah, Dangerous Swain, tell me no more,
Thy Happy Nymph you Worship and Adore!
When thy fill'd Eyes are sparkling at her Name,
I raving wish that mine had caus'd the Flame.

If by your fire to her you can impart
DiSffusive heat to warm another's heart;
Ah, dangerous Swain, what would the ruin be,
Should you but once persuade you burn for me!

*Mary De La Rivière Manley (1663-1724)*

# ON JEALOUSY

O shield me from his rage, celestial Powers!
This tyrant that embitters all my hours.
Ah, Love! you've poorly play'd the hero's part,
You conquer'd, but you can't defend my heart.
When first I bent beneath your gentle reign,
I thought this monster banish'd from your train:
But you would raise him to support your throne,
And now he claims your empire as his own;
Or tell me, tyrants, have you both agreed
That where one reigns, the other shall succeed?

*Esther Johnson (1681–1728)*

# JEALOUSY

'The myrtle bush grew shady
Down by the ford.'
'Is it even so?' said my lady.
'Even so!' said my lord.
'The leaves are set too thick together
For the point of a sword.

'The arras in your room hangs close,
No light between!
You wedded one of those that see unseen.'
'Is it even so?' said the King's Majesty.
'Even so!' said the Queen.


*Mary Elizabeth Coleridge (1861–1907)*

# COLDER

*He was six feet four, and forty-six*
*and even colder than he thought he was*
            —James Thurber, *The Thirteen Clocks*

Not that I cared about the other women.
Those perfumed breasts with hearts
of pure rock salt.
Lot's wives—
all of them.

I didn't care
if they fondled him at parties,
eased him in at home
between a husband & a child,
sucked him dry
with vacuum cleaner kisses.

It was the coldness that I minded,
though he'd warned me.
"I'm cold," he said—
(as if that helped any).
But he was colder
than he thought he was.

Cold sex.
A woman has to die
& be exhumed
four times a week
to know the meaning of it.

His hips are razors
his pelvic bones are knives,
even his elbows could cut butter.

Cold flows from his mouth
like a cloud of carbon dioxide.
His penis is pure dry ice
which turns to smoke.
His face hangs over my face—
an ice carving.

One of these days
he'll shatter
or
he'll melt.


*Erica Jong (b.1942)*


## From FELIX HOLT: THE RADICAL


This man's metallic; at a sudden blow
His soul rings hard. I cannot lay my palm,
Trembling with life, upon that jointed brass.
I shudder at the cold unanswering touch;
But if it press me in response, I'm bruised.


*George Eliot (1819-80)*

# TO MY RIVAL

Since you dare Brave me, with a Rivals Name,
You shall prevail, and I will quit my Claime:
For know, proud Maid, I Scorn to call him mine,
Whom thou durst ever hope to have made thine:
Yet I confess, I lov'd him once so well,
His presence was my Heav'n, his absence Hell:
With gen'rous excellence I fill'd his Brest,
And in sweet Beauteous Forms his Person drest;
For him I did Heaven, and its Pow'r despise,
And onely lived by th'Influence of his Eyes:
I fear'd not Rivals, for I thought that he
That was possess'd of such a Prize as me,
All meaner Objects wou'd Contemn, and Slight,
Nor let an abject thing Usurpe my Right:
But when I heard he was so wretched Base
To pay devotion to thy wrinkled Face
I Banish't him my sight, and told the Slave,
He had not Worth, but what my Fancy gave:
'Twas I that rais'd him to this Glorious State,
And can as easily Annihilate:
But let him live, Branded with Guilt and Shame,
And Shrink into the Shade from whence he came;
His Punishment shall be, the Loss of Me,
And be Augmented, by his gaining Thee.

'Ephelia' (fl.c.1678-82)

# A PETITION

Lady, whom my belovéd loves so well!
　　When on his clasping arm thy head reclineth,
When on thy lips his ardent kisses dwell,
　　And the bright flood of burning light that shineth
In his dark eyes, is pouréd into thine;
　　When thou shalt lie enfolded to his heart
　　In all the trusting helplessness of love;
　　If in such joy sorrow can find a part,
Oh, give one sigh unto a doom like mine!
　　Which I would have thee pity, but not prove.
One cold, calm, careless, wintry look that fell
　　Haply by chance on one, is all that he
Ever gave my love; round that, my wild thoughts dwell
　　In one eternal pang of memory.


*Frances Anne Kemble (1809-93)*

# THE OTHER WOMAN

She chooses her clothes in subdued colours
To suit a life rehearsed in the suburbs.
She rarely needs to appear in public—
Has no one to take her to the opera
Or out to a restaurant in the evening
While someone minds legitimate children.

His avenue paths are hung with lilac
Proud candles erect on the horse-chestnut
Laburnum dangling her gaudy earrings
Over into other people's gardens.
He has never dared to send her roses:
She buys herself flowers from street cor-
ners.

He comes to her flat while it is still light
And makes her curtain off the afternoon
So even then, she hardly sees his face.
Each week their liaison seems more unreal:
She raises her veil, the netted window—
Sees him vanish at the end of the street.


*Marion Lomax (b.1953)*

# THE HICKIE

I mouth
sorry in the mirror when I see
the mark I must have made just now
loving you.
Easy to say it's alright
adultery
like blasphemy is for believers but
even in our
situation simple etiquette says
love should leave us both unmarked.
You are on loan to me like a library book
and we both know it.
Fine if you love both of us
but neither of us must too much show it.

In my misted mirror
you trace two toothprints
on the skin of your shoulder and sure
you're almost quick enough
to smile out bright and clear for me
as if it was O.K.

Friends again, together in this bathroom
we finish washing love away.

*Liz Lochhead (b.1947)*

# SPILT MILK

Two soluble aspirins spore in this glass, their mycelia
fruiting the water, which I twist into milkiness.
The whole world seems to slide into the drain by my window.

It has rained and rained since you left, the streets black
and muscled with water. Out of pain and exhaustion you came
into my mouth, covering my tongue with your good and
    bitter milk.

Now I find you have cashed that cheque. I imagine you
slipping the paper under steel and glass. I sit here in a circle
of lamplight, studying women of nine hundred years past.

My hand moves into darkness as I write, *The adulterous woman
lost her nose and ears; the man was fined.* I drain the glass.
I still want to return to that hotel room by the station

to hear all night the goods trains coming and leaving.


*Sarah Maguire (b.1957)*

# STORY OF A HOTEL ROOM

Thinking we were safe—insanity!
We went in to make love. All the same
Idiots to trust the little hotel bedroom.
Then in the gloom . . .
. . . And who does not know that pair of shutters
With the awkward hook on them
All screeching whispers? Very well then, in the gloom
We set about acquiring one another
Urgently! But on a temporary basis
Only as guests—just guests of one another's senses.

But idiots to feel so safe you hold back nothing
Because the bed of cold, electric linen
Happens to be illicit . . .
To make love as well as that is ruinous.
Londoner, Parisian, someone should have warned us
That without permanent intentions
You have absolutely no protection
—If the act is clean, authentic, sumptuous,
The concurring deep love of the heart
Follows the naked work, profoundly moved by it.


*Rosemary Tonks (b.1932)*

# SYMPHONY RECITAL

I do not like my state of mind;
I'm bitter, querulous, unkind.
I hate my legs, I hate my hands,
I do not yearn for lovelier lands.
I dread the dawn's recurrent light;
I have to go to bed at night.
I snoot at simple, earnest folk.
I cannot take the gentlest joke.
I find no peace in paint or type.
My world is but a lot of tripe.
I'm disillusioned, empty-breasted.
I am not sick, I am not well.
My quondam dreams are shot to hell.
My soul is crushed, my spirit sore;
I do not like me any more.
I cavil, quarrel, grumble, grouse.
I ponder on the narrow house.
I shudder at the thought of men . . .
I'm due to fall in love again.

*Dorothy Parker (1893-1967)*

# THE FIRED POT

In our town, people live in rows.
The only irregular thing in a street is the steeple;
And where that points to, God only knows,
And not the poor disciplined people!

And I have watched the women growing old,
Passionate about pins, and pence, and soap,
Till the heart within my wedded breast grew cold,
And I lost hope.

But a young soldier came to our town,
He spoke his mind most candidly.
He asked me quickly to lie down,
And that was very good for me.

For though I gave him no embrace—
Remembering my duty—
He altered the expression of my face,
And gave me back my beauty.


*Anna Wickham (1884-1947)*

# NOT-LOVING

The spine doesn't give or arch to it.
It is brittle and stiff like dried sticks,
winter parchment.
Not-loving is spiky fingers scratching.
It is cracks and angles, not
smiling out of the round of the mouth and eyes.
There are no vegetables or flowers,
no fat baskets of wheat.
The barns are always empty and the sky is colourless—
not like any colours of water in East Anglia
or anywhere at all where lovers meet
like sky and water mirroring each other.
Not-loving is having nobody to miss
when you come out onto a station platform
for instance, heart beating,
nobody to run to suddenly, arms open,
as to the harvest or a festival of bright flowers.


*Sylvia Kantaris (b.1936)*

# THINKING OF LOVE

*That* desire is quite over
Or seems so as I lie
Using the sky as cover
And thinking of deep
Dreams unknown to a lover.

Being alone is now
Far from loneliness.
I can stretch and allow
Legs, arms, hands
Their complete freedom:
There is no-one to please.

But soon it comes—
Not simply the ache
Of a particular need,
But also the general hunger,
As if the flesh were a house
With too many empty
rooms.

*Elizabeth Jennings (b.1926)*

# HAIL, BLUSHING GODDESS,
# BEAUTEOUS SPRING!

Hail, blushing goddess, beauteous Spring!
Who, in thy jocund train dost bring
Loves and graces, smiling hours,
Balmy breezes, fragrant flowers;
Come, with tints of roseate hue,
Nature's faded charms renew.
    Yet why should I thy presence hail?
To me no more the breathing gale
Comes fraught with sweets, no more the rose
With such transcendant beauty blows,
As when Cadenus blest the scene,
And shared with me those joys serene.
When, unperceived, the lambent fire
Of friendship kindled new desire;
Still listening to his tuneful tongue,
The truths which angels might have sung
Divine impressed, their gentle sway,
And sweetly stole my soul away.
    My guide, instructor, lover, friend,
Dear names in one idea blend;
Oh! still conjoined, your incense rise,
And waft sweet odours to the skies.

*Esther Vanhomrigh (early 18th century)*

## CONVICTION (IV)

I like to get off with people,
I like to lie in their arms
I like to be held and lightly kissed,
Safe from all alarms.

I like to laugh and be happy
With a beautiful kiss,
I tell you, in all the world
There is no bliss like this.

*Stevie Smith (1902–71)*

## SO LONG

My man loved me so much
he wanted to kill me
cause he loved me so good
he wanted to die
cause he loved me without sorrow
so sad without tears
he loved me to kill to die to cry
so much he wanted to scream
cause I loved him too much I
drank his tears
loved him too much
I ate his strength
loved him too much I stole his joy
I loved him to drink to eat to steal
cause we loved so much
so good to love to love
so long to love
so long

*Jayne Cortez (b.1936)*

# MORE AND MORE

More and more frequently the edges
of me dissolve and I become
a wish to assimilate the world, including
you, if possible through the skin
like a cool plant's tricks with oxygen
and live by a harmless green burning.

I would not consume
you, or ever
finish, you would still be there
surrounding me, complete
as the air.

Unfortunately I don't have leaves.
Instead I have eyes
and teeth and other non-green
things which rule out osmosis.

So be careful, I mean it,
I give you a fair warning:

This kind of hunger draws
everything into its own
space; nor can we
talk it all over, have a calm
rational discussion.

There is no reason for this, only
a starved dog's logic about bones.


*Margaret Atwood (b.1939)*

# HE FUMBLES AT YOUR SOUL

He fumbles at your Soul
As Players at the Keys
Before they drop full Music on—
He stuns you by degrees—
Prepares your brittle Nature
For the Ethereal Blow
By fainter Hammers—further heard—
Then nearer—Then so slow
Your Breath has time to straighten—
Your Brain—to bubble Cool -
Deals—One—imperial—Thunderbolt—
That scalps your naked Soul—

When Winds take Forests in their Paws—
The Universe—is still—

*Emily Dickinson (1830-86)*

# EVADNE

I first tasted under Apollo's lips,
love and love sweetness,
I, Evadne;
my hair is made of crisp violets
or hyacinth which the wind combs back
across some rock shelf;
I, Evadne,
was made of the god of light.

His hair was crisp to my mouth,
as the flower of the crocus,
across my cheek,
cool as the silver-cress
on Erotos bank;
between my chin and throat,
his mouth slipped over and over.

Still between my arm and shoulder,
I feel the brush of his hair,
and my hands keep the gold they took,
as they wandered over and over,
that great arm-full of yellow flowers.

*H.D. (1886-1961)*

# NIGHT-PIECE

the moon has fallen on her back
night cannot console her thin belly
she ravens shadow

fires flicker and crumble
ash scudding lighter than snow

my hand a cupped moth clinging
in the folded dark our breath rises
a grey bird among pines

desire is formless between us
we are enormous as stars

last light withdraws over the sloping field
trees deep in their darker selves

your fingers stir in the black grass

memory of absence . . . . . . . . . .
the galloping shadow on the sky's rim

*Frances Horovitz (1938-83)*

# AIRING THE CHAPEL

We made our high bed in the low chapel
(Methodist of some kind, I forget which).
White sheets reflected in the slick varnish.
I never did like chapels, as I told you.
You agreed of course. We like them now,
for making love in. And the flowers!
They were all white that out-of-season—
snowdrops, lilies of the valley, cow parsley—
and two paired white butterflies.
When the preacher and his ladies visited
we feared for their devoutness
but they were only studying the cabbage whites.
They'd seen a lot of beds in the chapel, they said.
Lovers kept it aired and stopped the dry rot.
The man chatted man-to-man with you
about your job. I can't remember what it was.
In Manchester, I think? Anyway, that night
we made love gravely and with reverence
by candlelight and moths, and afterwards
admired our shadow-patterns in the aired varnish,
and the warm transparence of our fingertips.

*Sylvia Kantaris (b.1936)*

# CHINA

From behind he looks like a man
I once loved, that hang dog slouch
to his jeans, a sweater vest, his neck
thick veined as a horse cock, a halo
of chopped curls.

He orders coffee and searches
his pockets, first in front, then
from behind, a long finger sliding
into the slitted denim like that man
slipped his thumb into me one summer
as we lay after love, our freckled
bodies two plump starfish on the sheets.

Semen leaked and pooled in his palm
as he moved his thumb slowly, not
to excite me, just to affirm
he'd been there.

I have loved other men since, taken
them into my mouth like a warm vowel,
lay beneath them and watched their irises
float like small worlds in their opened eyes.

But this man pressed his thumb
toward the tail of my spine
like he was entering
China, or a ripe papaya
so that now when I think of love,
I think of this.

*Dorianne Laux*

# CONFIGURATIONS

He gives her all the configurations
of Europe.

She gives him a cloud burst of parrots.

He gives her straight blond hairs
and a white frenzy.

She gives him black wool.  The darkness
of her twin fruits.

He gives her uranium, platinum, aluminium
and concorde.

She gives him her 'Bantu buttocks'.

He rants about the spice in her skin.

She croons his alabaster and scratches him.

He does a Columbus—
falling on the shores of her tangled nappy orchard.

She delivers up the whole Indies again
But this time her wide legs close in
     slowly
Making a golden stool of the empire
of his head.


*Grace Nichols (b.1950)*

273

# THE WILLING MISTRISS

*Amyntas* led me to a Grove,
　　Where all the Trees did shade us;
The Sun it self, though it had Strove,
　　It could not have betray'd us:
The place secur'd from humane Eyes,
　　No other fear allows.
But when the Winds that gently rise,
　　Doe Kiss the yeilding Boughs.

Down there we satt upon the Moss,
　　And did begin to play
A Thousand Amorous Tricks, to pass
　　The heat of all the day.
A many Kisses he did give:
　　And I return'd the same
Which made me willing to receive
　　That which I dare not name.

His Charming Eyes no Aid requir'd
　　To tell their softning Tale;
On her that was already fir'd
　　'Twas Easy to prevaile.
He did but Kiss and Clasp me round,
　　Whilst those his thoughts Exprest:
And lay'd me gently on the Ground;
　　Ah who can guess the rest?

*Aphra Behn (1640-89)*

## AND AGAIN

The man with the big mouth
and the ribbon-elastic legs
has bowled me over

His tongue running in my mouth
is sweet as a bean

The bare branch of his forearm
sets me sweating
My pores open: no shelter

He's a dark man,
melancholic and bitter;
with a hornet's sting
he bites to the bone

Dreadful in suspicion,
he becomes a leech
—he will have me,
he sings it to the telephone wires

Since last year I've grown
cautious
and knowledgeable:
ruefully I refuse him

The child stamps and wails out,
mourning the trust of his fragrance—
the true skin,
indisputable
as jasmine in the dark

*Alison Fell (b.1944)*

# HE THAT NONE CAN CAPTURE

comes of own accord to me


The acrobat stride his swing in space
the pole rolled under his instep
catches the pits of his knees
is lipped by his triangled groin
fits the fold of his hard-carved buttocks

Long-thighed tight-hipped he drops
head-down and writhes erect
glazed smooth by speed a twirled top
sits immobile in the void

Gravity outwhipped squeezed like dough
is kneaded to his own design
a balance-egg at the plexus of his bowels
counteracting vertigo

Empty of fear and therefore without weight
he walks a wedge of steeper air
indifferent to the enormous stare
of onlookers in rims of awe below

Drumbeats are solid blocks beneath him
Strong brass horn-tones prolong him
on glittering stilts

Self-hurled he swims the color-stippled height
where nothing but whisks of light
can reach him

At night he is my lover


*May Swenson (b.1919)*

## From URANIA

Did I boast of liberty?
    'Twas an insolency vain
I do only look on thee,
    And I captive am again.


Lady Mary Wroth (?1586-?1640)

## MANY AND MORE

There are many and more
who would kiss my hand,
taste my lips,
to my loneliness lend
their bodies' warmth.

I have want of a friend.

There are few, some few,
who would give their names
and fortunes rich
or send first sons
to my ailing bed.

I have need of a friend.

There is one and only one
who will give the air
from his failing lungs
for my body's mend.

And that one is my love.

*Maya Angelou (b.1928)*

## DO YOU NOT KNOW THAT I NEED TO TOUCH YOU

Do you not know that I need to touch you
as I touch a fruit or child?

Knowledge I need of you that comes not with words.

Let me touch your hair, your moving lip,
the bone beneath the gentle skin.

I will not harm you—I do not want your sex.

Trust me to touch you and to leave you whole.


*Frances Horovitz (1938-83)*

# FRIENDSHIP AFTER LOVE

After the fierce midsummer all ablaze
    Has burned itself to ashes, and expires
    In the intensity of its own fires,
There come the mellow, mild, St. Martin days
Crowned with the calm of peace, but sad with haze.
    So after Love has led us, till he tires
    Of his own throes, and torments, and desires,
Comes large-eyed friendship: with a restful gaze,
He beckons us to follow, and across
    Cool verdant vales we wander free from care.
    Is it a touch of frost lies in the air?
Why are we haunted with a sense of loss?
We do not wish the pain back, or the heat;
And yet, and yet, these days are incomplete.

*Ella Wheeler Wilcox (1850-1919)*

## SO THIS IS LOVE

*"The real love that follows*
*early delight and ignorance.*
*A wonderful sad dance that comes after."*
                                    —Jack Gilbert


So this is love, a kind of sad dance
and who's leading? I lie in bed
without you, your side not slept in
and I don't care. It's over one more time
just like it's raining once again,
a cat dies, you get another. Call it
the same name, remember the generalities,
not the specifics of such small deaths.

It makes me smile how we said this
is different, we've never loved before,
not really *loved*, you know. So here I am
again, trying to work up some kind of anger,
trying to find a word that fits what I
no longer feel.

The cat we got two days ago lies on your pillow,
purrs like he's been there all his life.
Perhaps he has, it's hard to tell the difference.
The rain feels like yesterday's, the long silences,
the same old tired dance.


*Lorna Crozier (b.1948)*

# STOCKING UP

Winter shall not find me withered
like the grasshopper. I take care
to store the autumn riches
against the lean times.
The body wilts and the head blooms
inside, amongst crab-apples.
My shelves are lined with delicacies,
salted or preserved in vinegar.
I have spiced some bitter memories
with dark, piquant humour
and bottled my resentments
ready for a hard winter.
Instead of weeping over ash of roses
I have laid in intellectual things
to see us through the long, cold evenings.
You may acquire a taste for my
asperities and vinegar when we are old
together indoors behind drawn curtains,
warmed by little, fierce fires
kindled with dead everlastings,
enjoying the residual crackle and static
of our summer conflagrations.


*Sylvia Kantaris (b.1936)*

# SONNET FOR CHRISTMAS

I saw our golden years on a black gale,
our time of love spilt in the furious dust.
"O we are winter-caught, and we must fail,"
said the dark dream, "and time is overcast."
- And woke into the night; but you were there,
and small as seed in the wild dark we lay.
Small as a seed under the gulfs of air
is set the stubborn heart that waits for day.
I saw our love the root that holds the vine
in the enduring earth, that can reply,
"Nothing shall die unless for me it die.
Murder and hate and love alike are mine";
and therefore fear no winter and no storm
while in the knot of earth that root lies warm.

*Judith Wright (b.1915)*

# ONE FLESH

Lying apart now, each in a separate bed,
He with a book, keeping the light on late,
She like a girl dreaming of childhood,
All men elsewhere—it is as if they wait
Some new event: the book he holds unread,
Her eyes fixed on the shadows overhead.

Tossed up like flotsam from a former passion,
How cool they lie. They hardly ever touch,
Or if they do it is like a confession
Of having little feeling—or too much.
Chastity faces them, a destination
For which their whole lives were a preparation.

Strangely apart, yet strangely close together,
Silence between them like a thread to hold
And not wind in. And time itself's a feather
Touching them gently. Do they know they're old,
These two who are my father and my mother
Whose fire from which I came, has now grown cold?

*Elizabeth Jennings (b.1926)*

# AUTUMN

He told his life story to Mrs. Courtly
Who was a widow. 'Let us get married shortly',
He said. 'I am no longer passionate,
But we can have some conversation before it is too late.'

*Stevie Smith (1902-71)*

## KISS'D YESTREEN

Kiss'd yestreen, and kiss'd yestreen,
Up the Gallowgate, down the Green:
I've woo'd wi' lords, and woo'd wi' lairds,
I've mool'd* wi' carles and mell'd* wi' cairds,      *played
I've kiss'd wi' priests—'twas done i' the dark,      *meddled
Twice in my gown and thrice in my sark;*             *shirt
But priest, nor lord, nor loon can gie
Sic kindly kisses as he gae me.

*Anonymous*

# NOTES ON POETS

FLEUR ADCOCK (b.1934)
New Zealander; poet. Born in New Zealand, she spent her childhood partly there and partly in Britain. Returned to New Zealand 1947 to 1963, then emigrated to London. She is considered one of New Zealand's most important authors and won the New Zealand Book Award in 1984. Her books include: *The Scenic Route* (1974), *The Inner Harbour* (1979), *Selected Poems* (1983) and *The Incident Book* (1986); she also edited *The Faber Book of 20th Century Women's Poetry* (1987).

MAYA ANGELOU (b.1928)
Born Marguerite Johnson. American poet born in St Louis, Missouri. After her parents' marriage disintegrated, she and an older brother went to live with their paternal grandfather in Arkansas. In the 1950s she performed in nightclubs in San Francisco and New York; she appeared in a production of *Porgy and Bess* that toured Europe and Africa. By 1970, she was writer in residence at the University of Kansas and lecturer at Yale University. She first became well known for her autobiographical writings, notably: *I Know Why the Caged Bird Sings.* Her books of poetry include: *Just Give Me a Cool Drink of Water 'fore I Diiie* (1971), *Oh Pray My Wings Are Gonna Fit Me Well* (1975), *And Still I Rise* (1978), *Sheba Sings the Song* (1987) and *I Shall Not Be Moved* (1990).

MARION ANGUS (1866-1946)
Scottish poet born in Aberdeen, she spent her childhood in Arbroath where her father was a minister. She published six volumes of poetry in her lifetime; her *Selected Poems* appeared in 1950.

MARGARET ATWOOD (b.1939)
Canadian novelist, poet, critic and short story writer. Born in Ottawa, she is Canada's foremost author. Much of her early life was spent in the bush country of northern Ontario and Quebec. She has taught English in universities across Canada, and has received over twenty awards for her writing, including the Governor-General's Award for her first volume of poetry, *The Circle Game* (1966). She has published fourteen volumes of poetry, six novels and three collections of short stories to date, and now lives on a farm in south Ontario with the writer Graeme Gibson and their daughter. Selections of verse from most of her books appear in *Poems 1965-1975* (1976) and *Poems 1976-1986* (1987).

LADY GRIZEL HUME BAILLIE (1665-1746)
Scottish poet and day-book keeper. The eldest of eighteen children in a Presbyterian family whose political convictions led to their persecution towards the end of the Stuart reign. Her legendary bravery in saving her father's life was celebrated by her descendant Joanna Baillie in *Metrical Legends of Exalted Characters* (1821). The family went into exile in Utrecht, where Lady Grizel managed the household. After the Glorious Revolution in 1688, she

returned to Britain with the Prince of Orange, and was invited to become maid of honour at court, but refused, having already fallen in love with George Baillie, the son of one of her father's martyred friends. 'Werena My Heart Licht', long thought an excellent example of the Scottish ballad, probably comes from a book of songs published in Utrecht, of which no copies survive.

### JOANNA BAILLIE (1762-1851)

Scottish poet, dramatist and songwriter. Born in Lanarkshire, a descendant of Lady Grizel Baillie; her father was a clergyman, said to be repressive and stern. At ten she was sent to school in Glasgow. In 1784, on the death of her father, she and her mother and sisters moved to London. In 1790, Baillie's *Fugitive Verses* was published anonymously and favourably received. She remained single but had a wide circle of friends including Sir Walter Scott. The story of how her ancestor, Lady Grizel Baillie, saved her father from his persecutors by hiding him and bringing him food and drink at night appears in her *Metrical Legends* (1821); her *Collection of Poems* was published in 1823.

### MARTHA BAIRD (1921-81)

American poet. She was born in Dodge City, Kansas, in 1921. After graduating from the University of Iowa, she moved to New York City in 1943 to study the philosophy Aesthetic Realism with its founder, the American poet and critic Eli Siegel. Baird began writing poetry while attending Eli Siegel's classes. 'It was as if the shutters were taken off the windows of my soul' she wrote. In 1944, Siegel and Baird were married. Baird's first book, *Nice Deity*, was published in 1955; other poems are included in *Personal and Impersonal: Six Aesthetic Realists* (1959). Baird wrote on a wide variety of subjects, including music, Homer's Iliad and the contemporary novel; she also worked as an editor for Definition Press, principally on books by and about her husband and Aesthetic Realism.

### MARY BARBER (c.1690-1757)

Irish poet. She was married to a woollen draper who had moved to Dublin from England; the couple had four children. She published a few poems in Dublin in the 1720s. In 1730 she travelled to England, visiting London, Tunbridge Wells and Bath. She impressed Jonathan Swift with her verse, and he helped her to assemble a list of subscribers for her *Poems on Several Occasions*, which was published in 1734. She remained in England for a few more years, suffering increasingly from rheumatism and gout. In the 1740s she travelled back to live in Ireland again, probably with one of her children.

### JANE BARKER (1652-C.1727)

English poet born into a Royalist family in Northamptonshire. Her early poems were well received by her brother (of whom she was very fond) and his friends, then at St John's College, Oxford, who compared her work favourably with that of Katherine Philips. In the late 1670s, both her father and brother died, and she spent a lonely fifteen years in the company of her mother, who died in 1685. Just after her *Poetical Recreations* was published in 1688, she went into exile in France with James II, returning to England during the reign of Queen Anne. She went back to France in about 1727, and probably died there.

PATRICIA BEER (b.1924)

English poet, critic and novelist born in the West Country where she has
spent most of her life. After graduating from St Hugh's College, Oxford,
she spent seven years teaching in Italy, and then taught at Goldsmiths College,
London (1962-68). She has published at least eight volumes of poetry and
one novel; her *Collected Poems* was published in 1988.

APHRA BEHN (1640-89)

Playwright, poet, translator and novelist – the first professional woman
writer in England. Her early life remains fairly obscure. She was probably
born in Kent, and it has been deduced from her novel, *Oroonoko*, that she
travelled to Surinam, probably in 1663-64. Those piecing together her biography
conclude that, on her return to London, she probably married a Dutch mer-
chant called Behn, who may almost immediately have fallen victim to the
plague. There is firm evidence that in 1666 she was sent to Antwerp as a
spy for the English government, charged with obtaining information on
Dutch military plans and Cromwellians living in exile. Her code name was
Astrea, which she later adopted as a pen-name. After a spell in a debtors'
prison in the Netherlands (she had run out of money), she returned to
London, where she became known among her wide circle of friends for her
wit and generosity. Her tendency to outspoken criticism provoked bitter
personal and political attacks on her, and her robust style of writing, which
was thought more appropriate to a man, also excited strong disapproval. In
her later years she was poverty-stricken, ill and disillusioned. Seventeen of
her plays survive; she was the first woman whose writing won her burial in
Westminster Abbey.

STELLA BENSON (1892-1933)

English novelist, poet and short story writer born in Shropshire. She did
charity work in London's East End (1913-17), and was active as a suf-
fragette. On her way back from an 18-month trip to America (1918-20), via
India and China, she met and fell in love with a customs officer James
O'Gorman Anderson, whom she married in 1921. She spent most of the rest
of her life in China, where her husband's work dictated that they live, and
died of pneumonia there. Her work that received wide acclaim in her life-
time was *Tobit Transplanted*. Her *Poems* was published in 1935.

ANN BERESFORD (b.1919)

English poet born in Redhill, Surrey, who married Michael Hamburger in
1951, separated from him, then remarried him in 1974. Her highly active life
has included working as a broadcaster for the BBC, teaching drama and poetry,
being a musician and actress and writing over a dozen volumes of poetry.

LOUISA S. BEVINGTON (b.1845)

English poet. The eldest of eight children. Her father was a Quaker, who
encouraged her to write and pursue an interest in nature. She wrote articles
and poetry on the theme of evolutionism. In 1883, she married an artist
from Munich, Ignatz Guggenberger, and lived with him first in Meran,
then in London. Her books include: *Key-Notes* (1876, 1879), *Poems, Lyrics and
Sonnets* (1882) and *Liberty Lyrics* (1895).

## SUSANNA BLAMIRE (1747-94)

English poet and songwriter. Known as the 'Muse of Cumberland' in her own day, when she was highly thought of. Blamire remained single and lived a quiet life in and around Carlisle with her family until her death from some kind of rheumatoid condition. Several of her poems were published anonymously in various journals, but most of her work was written without firm plans for publication. An anthology of her poems was first collected and published in 1842 by Patrick Maxwell, an Englishman living in India, and Henry Lonsdale, a Carlisle physician.

## MATHILDE BLIND (1841-96)

Poet, biographer, translator and editor. Born in Mannheim, Germany. Her stepfather was a political writer and revolutionary, whose activities forced him and his family to flee first to Belgium and then, in about 1851/52, to London. Their home became a meeting place for political refugees, among them Garibaldi and Mazzini. Blind was a highly independent young woman, travelling on her own through Switzerland at the age of 18. She moved into her own home at the age of 30 and travelled through England, Europe and to Egypt, after coming into a legacy from her brother who had committed suicide in prison (he had tried to assassinate Bismarck). Blind's first volume of *Poems* was published in 1867 under a pseudonym, Claude Lake.

## LILIAN BOWES LYON (1895-1949)

English poet. Published five volumes of poetry. Her *Collected Poems* was published in 1948.

## ANNE BRADSTREET (?1613-72)

English woman born in Lincolnshire, who is nevertheless identified as the first American poet because she had settled in America by the time she began to write. She was educated in a solidly Puritan household, but read poetry when young. She and her husband lived on the estate of the Countess of Warwick (where he was employed) until they emigrated with Anne's parents to America in 1630. The couple had eight children between 1634 and 1652 and during this time Bradstreet wrote poetry, which was published anonymously under the title, *The Tenth Muse lately sprung up in America*, in 1650.

## EMILY BRONTË (1818-48)

English novelist and poet. Her fame rests on a single novel, *Wuthering Heights* (1847), and a small number of poems. She was the fifth child in the family; her mother died before she was three. Like her sisters, Charlotte and Anne, she wrote a great deal from an early age. Charlotte discovered Emily's poetry (which had been written in secret) in 1845, and it was almost all published the following year in a joint publication of all three sisters' work under the pseudonyms Acton, Currer and Ellis Bell. Emily seems to have been less than delighted at her poetry being made public, and was uninterested in receiving any publicity. She died of tuberculosis, refusing to accept any medical help.

## ELIZABETH BARRETT BROWNING (1806-61)

English poet and novelist. Born in Durham and brought up in Herefordshire. The eldest of twelve children, she was encouraged by both parents to read a great deal, apparently learnt to read Greek at the age of eight and was taught by her brothers' tutors. Her first volume of poems was privately published when she was 14. Shortly after this, she suffered her first attack of a nervous and pulmonary disorder which was to plague her from then on, forcing her to live as an invalid for long periods. Her mother died when she was twenty. In 1838 a personal tragedy struck for which she was to feel guilty and responsible for the rest of her life: sent to Torquay to recuperate from a lung haemorrhage, she insisted (against her father's wishes) on being accompanied by her beloved brother, who drowned in a sailing accident. In 1844 her first successful book, *Poems*, appeared, and caught the attention of Robert Browning. Her father had made it plain that he was against the idea of her marrying, so Browning's courtship of Elizabeth was secret, as was their marriage in 1846; a week after the ceremony the couple fled to Italy. Elizabeth's father never forgave her. The couple settled in Florence and in 1849 had a son. Her *Sonnets from the Portuguese* (1850) express her love for her husband, *Aurora Leigh* (1857) consolidated her reputation. She died unexpectedly in 1861, writing poetry to the end. *Last Poems* was published posthumously.

### AMELIA JOSEPHINE BURR (b.1878)
American poet. Educated at Hunter College, New York, she produced four volumes of poetry, including *In Deep Places*, from which the poem in this collection is taken.

### LADY SOPHIA BURRELL (?1750-1802)
English poet and dramatist. Elder daughter of a wealthy banker from Essex. When, in 1773, she married an advocate, William Burrell, Director of the South Sea Company and MP, she took with her a fortune of £100,000. The couple had five sons and two daughters; after her husband had a stroke, they moved to Deepdene in Surrey. She wrote poetry throughout her marriage, some addressed directly to friends. Her husband died in 1796, and the following year she married a clergyman and moved to the Isle of Wight, where she died aged about 52. Her *Poems* was published in 1793.

### LADY MARY CHUDLEIGH (1656-1710)
English poet and essayist. Born and brought up in Devon. She married Sir George Chudleigh of Ashton, Devon, and bore two sons and a daughter; the latter died young, provoking Chudleigh to write a heart-rending poem on the subject. She had a wide knowledge of poetry, history, philosophy and theology, and was part of a circle of literary women with similar training and ideas, to some of whom various of her poems were addressed, using classical pseudonyms – a convention of the time. She was an admirer of the feminist Mary Astell. Her *The Ladies' Defence* (1701), published anonymously, was a spirited response to a misogynist sermon called *The Bride Womans Counsellor*, published in 1699 by John Sprint, a Nonconformist minister.

### CATHERINE COCKBURN (1679-1749)
After the death of her father, who was a sea captain, Cockburn's family was poor, and she began writing for publication at the age of 14 to help support them. She wrote five plays and also published (anonymously) a novel.

### MARY ELIZABETH COLERIDGE (1861-1907)
English poet, novelist and critic. Great-great-niece of Samuel Taylor Coleridge.

born in London and educated at home. Her parents had a wide circle of literary and artistic friends including Tennyson, Browning, Ruskin, Millais the painter and the actress Fanny Kemble. Tutored by a friend of her father, Coleridge learned six languages including Greek and Hebrew. She remained single, living at the family home, but travelled abroad with four female friends. She was sensitised to the plight of the poor by reading Tolstoy, and taught working women first in her own home and then, 1895-1907, at a Working Women's College. Her literary reputation was established by the publication of her novel, *The King with Two Faces* (1897). She was unsure about publishing her poetry until Robert Bridges read it and encouraged her to do so. She still did not allow it to be published under her name, preferring to remain anonymous or to adopt a Greek pseudonym meaning 'The Wanderer'. She died at the age of 45 of appendicitis. Her *Collected Poems* was published in 1954.

### GRACE HAZARD CONKLING (late 19th/early 20th century)
American poet. The poem in this collection, was found in an anthology compiled by Sara Teasdale and published in the United States in 1917.

### WENDY COPE (b.1945)
English poet. Born in Kent. She read history at St Hilda's College, Oxford. Her first full-length collection of poetry was *Making Cocoa for Kingsley Amis* (1986), and she won a Cholmondeley Award for poetry in 1987. Her most recent collection is *Serious Concerns*. She now lives in London.

### ALICE CORBIN (late 19th/early 20th century)
American poet. Actually Alice Corbin Henderson. She was Associate Editor of *Poetry: A Magazine of Verse* 1912-17, before developing tuberculosis. The poem in this collection was found in an anthology compiled by Sara Teasdale and published in the United States in 1917.

### FRANCES CORNFORD (1886-1960)
English poet and translator. Grand-daughter of Charles Darwin, daughter of Sir Francis and his second wife. She was educated at home. She married Francis Macdonald Cornford, a Fellow of Trinity College, Cambridge, and had five children. Her first volume of poetry (of which she produced nine) appeared in 1910; her *Collected Poems* appeared in 1954, and a final book, *A Calm Shore*, was published in the last year of her life.

### JAYNE CORTEZ (b.1936)
American poet born in Arizona. She has lectured in and read poetry at many institutions in the United States and West Africa. She is the author of several volumes of poetry, including: *Piss-stained Stairs and the Monkey Man's Wares* (1969) and *Coagulations: New and Selected Poems* (1984).

### DINAH MARIA MULOCK CRAIK (1826-87)
English poet born in Stoke on Trent. Craik was a prolific and popular Victorian author who began writing to support herself and her two young brothers. After her marriage, she continued to write in spite of her husband's objections. A volume of her collected poems, entitled *Thirty Years: Poems Old and New*, was published in 1880.

LORNA CROZIER (b.1948)
Canadian poet. Born and brought up in Swift Current, Saskatchewan. She has taught at the University of Saskatoon and now teaches at the University of Victoria in British Columbia where she lives. Eight volumes of her poetry have been published, the most recent of which is *Inventing the Hawk* (1992), which won the Governor-General's Award for Poetry.

NORA B. CUNNINGHAM (late 19th/early 20th century)
American poet. The poem in this collection is taken from the December 1923 edition of *Poetry: A Magazine of Verse*, published in Chicago.

CATHERINE LUCY CZERKAWSKA (b.1950)
Poet and writer of short stories and radio plays. Born in Leeds, she now lives in Scotland. Her first volume of poetry, *White Boats*, was produced in collaboration with Andrew Greig in 1973; *A Book of Men and other poems* was published in 1976.

ANN DARR
American poet born in Iowa. She now lives near Washington D.C. She was a pilot in the US Army Airforce during World War II, has been a writer and performer for radio in New York and teaches at American University in Washington D.C. Her seventh book of poetry was published in 1993.

MARY CAROLYN DAVIES (late 19th/early 20th century)
American poet, whose poem 'Love Song', included in this book, was published in an anthology of love poetry compiled by Sara Teasdale and published in the United States in 1917.

BABETTE DEUTSCH (b.1895)
American poet, novelist, translator, critic and writer for children. Born in New York, of German descent. She was married to Avrahm Yarmolinsky. She graduated from Barnard College in 1917. In the early 1950s, she taught at Columbia University. Her first volume of poetry, *Banners*, was published in 1919 and four others followed by 1954. Her *Collected Poems 1919-62* appeared in 1967.

EMILY DICKINSON (1830-86)
American poet born in Amherst, Massachusetts. Her family were descendants of a religious dissenter who settled in Connecticut in 1630. Her father was a Massachusetts judge; Dickinson's mother was a semi-invalid. She attended Amherst Academy and Mount Holyoke Female Seminary. Her health was fragile. Except for an occasional visit to nearby cities and a trip to Washington D.C. with her father, Dickinson scarcely ever left her parents' home and lived there after their death, becoming a legendary figure locally, an eccentric spinster who dressed in white, would not go outside her own house and garden and rarely received visitors. She read, corresponded with a few friends and wrote poems. After she died, her sister found hundreds of poems in a box in her room, many scribbled on scrap bits of paper. Only seven had been published in Dickinson's lifetime. The first edition of some of her work appeared in 1890, and various others followed through the 1930s. A full, scholarly edition containing 1775 poems was finally published in 1955.

SARAH DIXON (fl.1716-45)
English poet. Her *Poems on Several Occasions* was published anonymously in Canterbury in 1740, and it has been deduced from inscriptions in some copies that she was a widow living in the town. Among the subscribers to the volume, who were predominantly local, were Edward Cave, Elizabeth Carter and Alexander Pope.

MAURA DOOLEY (b.1957)
Born in Ireland; now living in England. She organised writers' courses at an arts centre in Yorkshire for five years, and in 1987 became Literature Officer of London's South Bank Centre. She won a Gregory Award in 1987. Her first two, short collections were *Ivy Leaves & Arrows* (1986) and *Turbulence* (1988); *Explaining Magnetism*, her first full-length collection, was published in 1992.

HILDA DOOLITTLE (1886-1961)
Wrote as 'H.D.' American poet, essayist, translator, dramatist, film critic and novelist. Born in Bethlehem, Pennsylvania. Daughter of a professor of astronomy and descendant of one of the members of the original Moravian Brotherhood, an 18th-century mystical order - she was deeply affected by their ritual beliefs. She was briefly engaged to Ezra Pound before emigrating to London in 1911, rarely returning to the United States thereafter. She married the British poet Richard Aldington in 1913, but separated from him five years later. She produced thirteen volumes of poetry; her reputation was established by her *Collected Poems*, published in 1925.

LADY DOROTHEA DU BOIS (1728-74)
English poet, novelist and dramatist. Born in Ireland, the eldest daughter of Richard Annesley, Lord Altham. In 1737 he became Earl of Anglesey, and three years later he abandoned his wife and declared his three daughters illegitimate, marrying instead Juliana Donovan, the daughter of a Wexford merchant. His extraordinary defence was that the marriage to Dorothea's mother had been bigamous (on his part) and was therefore invalid. Dorothea made a clandestine marriage to a French musician in about 1752 and bore six children. She waged a long and unsuccessful campaign to force her father to acknowledge her mother, herself and her siblings as his true family, and during the 1760s began to write to support her family. Her *Poems on Several Occasions* (Dublin, 1764) included an autobiographical poem describing her father's behaviour, and she repeated her claims in various other forms. She died in Dublin in 1774, knowing that all her efforts to right the injustices of the past had been in vain.

CAROL ANN DUFFY (b.1955)
Born in Scotland, she now lives and works in London. Her first collection of poems, *Standing Female Nude* (1983), won first prize in the National Poetry Competition, Scottish Arts Council Book Awards of Merit; it has also won many other awards. Other poetry collections include *Selling Manhattan* (1987) and *The Other Country* (1990).

MAUREEN DUFFY (b.1933)
English novelist, poet and dramatist. She read English at King's College, London, and worked as a schoolteacher for five years. She co-founded the

Writers' Action Group in 1972; since 1985, she has been President of the Writers' Guild and has been a powerful voice in the Public Lending Right campaign. Her *Collected Poems 1949-84* was published in 1985.

### LADY CATHERINE DYER (d.1654)
English poet. No verse by her is known except for the epitaph to her husband on a gravestone in Colmworth Church, Bedfordshire.

### GEORGE ELIOT (1819-80)
Pseudonym of Mary Ann Evans. English novelist, essayist, poet. Daughter of a Warwickshire farm manager, of strong Protestant conviction. While at school, she was greatly influenced by the evangelical fervour of some of her teachers. In her twenties, however, she came to know the free-thinker Charles Bray, whose beliefs probably contributed to her later adoption of humanism. After her mother's death in 1836, she looked after her father until he died in 1849, after which she went to Geneva for a while, then returned to London and for two years edited (though not in name) the *Westminster Review*. A romantic liaison with a writer called George Henry Lewes began, complicated by the fact that he could not obtain a divorce from his wife in spite of her relationship with another man by whom she had several children; Lewes supported them all. Eliot and Lewes went to Weimar in Germany for eight months, an action that led to her estrangement from her brother and from many of her women friends, who were horrified by the scandal. Their quasi marriage lasted 24 years until Lewes's death in 1878, and all her significant work was produced during this time: seven novels, a verse drama and a collection of essays. In 1879, she finally entered into legal marriage with John Walker Cross, a man twenty years her junior, but lived only seven months to enjoy the union.

### 'ELIZA' (fl.1652)
English poet who was author of *Eliza's Babes: or The Virgins-Offering*, published in London in 1652. She is described on the title page as 'a Lady, who onely desires to advance the glory of God, and not her own'. The book is dedicated to her sisters, and three poems talk of a brother who was ill and died.

### QUEEN ELIZABETH I (1533-1603)
English poet, devotional writer and orator. When she was three, her mother, Ann Boleyn, was executed on the orders of her father, Henry VIII, who himself had died. At 25, having undergone imprisonment in the Tower during the reign of Mary, she became Queen of England and Ireland (in 1558). Two prominent Protestant scholars, Roger Ascham and William Grindel, directed her early education. Elizabeth cultivated an interest in history and classical literature and showed a considerable facility with modern languages, which enabled her to deal directly with foreign emissaries. She was expert enough in French, Italian, Latin and Greek to write a book of devotions in these four languages, as well as English. Many poems have traditionally been ascribed to her, but only a handful are now believed to have been written by her.

### 'EPHELIA' (fl.c.1678-82)
The identity of this English poet remains a mystery. She is the author of *Female Poems on Several Occasions Written by Ephelia* (1679, 1682), one of the earliest

recorded collections of poetry by an English woman. Scholars of the period reckon that she was born about 1650. She refers to the early deaths of both parents leaving her destitute. The 'J.G.' to whom some of her lyrics are addressed is believed to have been a gold trader, involved in Crown interests in Tangier, where, perhaps, he found and married Ephelia's 'Rival'.

### JULIANA HORATIA EWING (1841-85)

English writer for children. Born in Ecclesfield, Yorkshire, her father was a clergyman. She produced many children's stories, often illustrated by well-known artists including Randolph Caldecott and George Cruikshank. She married an army major in 1829, lived for two years in Canada and then in various parts of England, where she remained when her husband was posted to Malta and Ceylon, because of fragile health. Her book *The Brownies* (1870) inspired Baden-Powell to use the name for the junior section of the Girl Guides.

### CATHERINE MARIA FANSHAWE (1765-1834)

English poet whose health was weak, and who is said to have been 'deformed in body'. She lived most of her life travelling in southern Europe: painting, etching, sketching (particularly in Italy) and writing verses. Her poems were first published in the *Collection* put together by Joanna Baillie that appeared in 1823.

### VICKI FEAVER (b.1943)

English poet born in Nottinghamshire. She read music at Durham University. The poem in this collection is from her first publication, *Close Relatives* (1981).

### ALISON FELL (b.1944)

Scottish poet, novelist and children's writer. Born in Dumfries. She trained as a sculptor, then became involved in women's street theatre groups and contributed articles to various journals including *Spare Rib* and *Time Out*. She now lives in London. *Kisses for Mayakovsky* won the Alice Hunt Bartlett prize for poetry in 1984. Other volumes of poetry include *Bread and Roses* (1982) and *Crystal Owl* (1988).

### MICHAEL FIELD (1846-1914 & 1862-1913)

The name conceals the identity of two English poets and playwrights, Katherine Harris Bradley (1846-1914) and Edith Emma Cooper (1862-1913). After Bradley joined the household of her invalid older sister, Cooper's mother, she took over the care and education of her young niece. In 1878 they all moved to Bristol where Bradley and Cooper went to University College together. They both joined debating societies and women's suffrage organisations, and pursued anti-vivisectionist activities. By the time Cooper reached the age of 20, they had declared themselves to be 'Against the world, to be/Poets and lovers evermore.' They collaborated on twenty-five tragic dramas and eight volumes of poetry. They died of cancer within a few months of each other.

### ANN FINCH, COUNTESS OF WINCHILSEA (1661-1720)

English poet. Her father, Sir William Kingsmill, died before she was born; her mother and stepfather died while she was still a child. She became maid of honour to Mary of Modena (wife of James II), and later married a

Court officer, Colonel Heneage Finch. When James II fled to France, the couple moved to the seat of the Earl of Winchilsea in Kent, and Finch's husband inherited the title in 1712. A friend of Pope, Gay and other men of letters, she published anonymously (*Miscellany Poems on Several Occasions Written by a Lady*, 1713). In 1815, Wordsworth brought her by then entirely neglected work to public attention in an anthology, and a comprehensive edition of her work was published in 1903 by Chicago University Press.

HELEN FOLEY (1896-1937)
English poet. She went to Newnham College, Cambridge and graduated in medieval and modern languages in 1919. After a six-month secretarial course, she worked in London until 1921, for some time as an indexer for the League of Nations staff. In 1924, she married H.A. St George Saunders. She had three children, one of whom died in infancy. Her *Poems* was published in 1938.

KATH FRASER (b.1947)
English poet, born in London. Trained as a clinical psychologist, then worked as a gardener. The poem in this collection was found in *One Foot on the Mountain. An anthology of British feminist poetry 1969-1979* (ed. Lilian Mohin, 1979).

JEAN GARRIGUE (1912-72)
American poet. Born Gertrude Louise Garrigus in Evansville, Indiana. She was brought up in Indianapolis and educated at the universities of Chicago and Iowa. In about 1940 she moved to New York and it was here that she changed her name. A number of her poems were first published in a journal in 1941. In the 1950s, she taught in various establishments of higher education, including the University of Connecticut and Smith. In 1971, while teaching on the West Coast, Garrigue fell seriously ill and died a year later of Hodgkin's disease. Her books include: *The Ego and the Centaur* (1947), *The Monument Rose* (1953). Her *Collected Poems* was published in 1992.

KAREN GERSHON (b.1923)
English poet. She came to England at the age of fifteen in the winter before the outbreak of World War II en route for Palestine, but the war prevented her from going there. Her work was first published in 1959. Her *Collected Poems* was published in 1990.

STELLA GIBBONS (b.1902)
English novelist, journalist, poet. Born in London. Her father was a doctor. Gibbons studied journalism at University College London, a profession that she followed for ten years before writing fiction and poetry became her primary occupation. In 1933 she married Allan Bourne Webb (an actor and singer), who died in 1959. She has one daughter. Her *Collected Poems* was published in 1951. She is best known for her first novel, *Cold Comfort Farm*, for which she was awarded the Femina Vie Heureuse Prize in 1934.

MARY GILMORE (1865-1962)
Australian poet, journalist and essayist. Born at Cottawalla, in southern New South Wales. As a schoolchild she became a pupil-teacher at a school in Wagga Wagga, and subsequently taught in the mining area of Broken Hill. In 1890 she went to Sydney, where she moved in literary circles and

formed a close attachment to Henry Lawson, a highly respected writer. In 1896 she participated in an attempt by William Lane to set up an ideal socialist community in Cosme, Paraguay, where she met and married a sheep shearer called William Gilmore. They returned to Australia in 1902. In 1908 Gilmore took on the editorship of the women's page of *Australian Worker*, a Sydney newspaper, in which she campaigned for numerous welfare causes, including old age and invalid pensions, maternity allowances, the rights of illegitimate and adopted children and the rights of the Aborigines. A founder member of the Fellowship of Australian Writers, she was appointed a Dame Commander of the Order of the British Empire for services to literature in 1937. Her books include: *Marri'd and other Verses* (1910), *The Passionate Heart* (1918), *The Tilted Cart* (1925), *The Wild Swan* (1930), *The Rue Tree* (1931), *Under the Wilgas* (1932) and *Old Days, Old Ways* (1934).

LOUISE GLUCK (b.1943)
American poet. Born in New York City. Her books include: *Firstborn* (1969), *The House on Marshland* (1975), *Descending Figure* (1980) and *The Triumph of Achilles* (1985).

FRANCES GREVILLE (?1724-89)
English poet. The seventh of nine children of James and Catherine Coote Macartney of Longford, Ireland. Her mother died in 1731. In 1747, she married Fulke Greville of Wiltshire, who turned out to be a spendthrift who lived wildly beyond his means and was fond of gambling. They went to France in 1749, returning to Wiltshire in 1753, and the family was gradually ruined by Fulke Greville's extravagant habits. Mrs Greville's famous 'Ode to Indifference' (from which an extract has been taken for this book) was supposed to have been provoked by the death of her son and the continuing disastrous behaviour of her husband. Despite her considerable talent, she dared not publish her writings, partly because the convention of the time would have found it unfitting for a woman of her standing, but also because her husband objected violently to the idea. Friends to whom she wrote were given strict instructions never to reveal the rare pieces of verse included in the letters. She came into a small inheritance from her father and spent the rest of her life successfully arranging for her children's future (she bore seven, of whom four survived) and preventing her husband from getting his hands on her modest income. She finally managed to secure a legal separation from her husband in the mid-1780s, but her health was by this time broken and she died soon after.

MRS. FLEETWOOD HABERGHAM (d.1703)
Little is known about this English poet. The poem included in this book was taken from *The Delightful New Academy of Compliments*, published c.1765.

GWEN HARWOOD (b.1920)
Australian poet born in Brisbane, Queensland. She is an organist and has taught music in Brisbane. She has published several collections of poetry, and has won a number of awards for her verse. Her *Collected Poems* was published in 1991.

PHOEBE HESKETH (b.1909)
English poet, journalist and writer for television. Born in Preston. She

married in 1931, had three children and lived for many years in Rivington, Lancashire. Her first book appeared in 1948. A selection from her ten books of poetry together with new and previously unpublished poems entitled *Netting the Sun* was published in 1989.

FRANCES HOROVITZ (1938-83)
English poet. Born in London, she was educated at Bristol University and the Royal Acadamy of Dramatic Art. She frequently read poetry for the BBC and the Open University. She was married to the poet Michael Horovitz by whom she had one son. She subsequently married the critic Roger Garfitt. Her books include: *Water Over Stone* (1980) and *Snow Light, Water Light* (1983). Her *Collected Poems* was published in 1985.

HELEN MARIA HUNT JACKSON (1830-85)
American poet and novelist. Born in Amherst, Massachusetts, she married Edward Hunt in 1852 (he died in 1863). She published two volumes of verse, two novels and a commentary entitled *A Century of Dishonor* (1881) which recorded government wrongdoings in dealing with the Indians and led directly to her appointment in 1882 as special commissioner to investigate conditions among the Mission Indians of California. Her books of poetry were *Verses* (1870) and *Sonnets and Lyrics* (1886).

ELIZABETH JANE JENNINGS (b.1926)
English poet. Born in Lincolnshire and educated at Oxford, where she now lives. She received the Somerset Maugham Award in 1956. Her *Collected Poems* was published in 1967, since when she has published further volumes of poetry including: *The Animals' Arrival* (1969), *Lucidities* (1970), *Consequently I Rejoice* (1977), *Moments of Grace* (1979) and *Celebrations and Elegies* (1982). Her *Collected Poems* was published in 1970 and *Selected Poems* in 1979.

ESTHER JOHNSON (1681-1728)
English poet. A member, with Jonathan Swift, of the household of the diplomat and essayist, Sir William Temple. Swift's *Journal to Stella* was addressed to Esther Johnson.

ERICA JONG (b.1942)
American novelist and poet. Born in New York City, the second of three daughters, she grew up on Manhattan's Upper West Side. She won a number of awards for her writing while an undergraduate at Columbia University, and from 1966 to 1969 taught in Germany at Heidelberg. *Fear of Flying*, her first novel, made her a celebrity. She has published several volumes of poetry; *Loveroot* (1975) won several awards. Other books of poetry include: *Fruits and Vegetables* (1971), *Half Lives* (1973).

SYLVIA KANTARIS (b.1936)
English poet. Born in the Peak District, Derbyshire. She read French at Bristol University, taught in Bristol and London, then spent ten years in Australia, where she taught French at Queensland University. She returned to England to settle in Helston, Cornwall, in 1974 and from 1975 to 1984 worked for the Open University, as a tutor in twentieth-century poetry. In 1986, she was appointed Cornwall's first Writer in the Community. Her seven books to date include *The Tenth Muse* (1983) and, in 1989, *Dirty Washing,*

a selection of poetry from most of her previous publications together with a substantial number of new poems. Her most recent title is *Lad's Love* (1993).

## FRANCES ANNE KEMBLE (1809-93)

English actress (known as Fanny Kemble), poet, dramatist, autobiographer. Born into a prominent theatrical family, she was niece of the well-known actress Sarah Siddons. Financial difficulties led her father to ask her to take to the stage. On tour in America, she met and married a Philadelphian plantation owner. The marriage was not happy, partly because of their incompatible personalities, but also due to Kemble's distress once she realised that her husband's wealth was founded on slave-ownership. Having once visited his plantations in Georgia, she wrote and published, much to his and his family's chagrin, a bitter attack on slavery, *Journal of a Residence on a Georgian Plantation* (1863). The couple had separated, and Kemble travelled back to England, leaving behind her two daughters. She reappeared briefly on the stage, but then took up a successful career of public readings across Europe and America. She retired to Philadelphia to live close to her by then married children, but in 1877 returned to England once again.

## ANNE KILLIGREW (1660-85)

English poet and painter. Her father was the theologian Dr Henry Killigrew, chaplain to the Duke of York, and her uncles, the popular Royalist dramatists Thomas and Sir William Killigrew. Anne Killigrew was maid of honour to Mary of Modena, Duchess of York; one of her companions was Ann Finch, Countess of Winchilsea. Her contemporaries seem to have thought highly of her. Dryden said of her, 'Such noble vigour did her verse adorn,/That it seem'd borrow'd where 'twas only born.' Her father arranged for the publication of her poetry a year after her death from smallpox.

## DORIANNE LAUX

American poet. Lives in Berkeley, California. Her work has been widely published in magazines, and she was the winner of a 1987 Pushcart Prize. Some of her poems were published in a collection entitled *Three West Coast Women*, by Five Fingers Poetry, San Francisco, in 1987.

## SUE LENIER (b.1957)

English poet and playwright. Born in Birmingham. She went to school on Tyneside, and won a place at Cambridge University in 1977, graduating in 1980. In 1981-83, she held a Harkness Fellowship in the United States. Her book, *Swansongs*, was published in 1982; *Rain Following* was published in 1983.

## CHARLOTTE LENNOX (1729-1804)

English novelist and poet. Daughter of an army officer who obtained an appointment in New York Province and moved his family there. He died in about 1743, and Lennox returned to England, where two 'noble ladies' became her patrons. In 1747 she married Alexander Lennox and published *Poems on Several Occasions*. She later became a prolific novelist. Her marriage is said to have been unhappy. Her husband treated her harshly, and they probably separated permanently in 1792. She had a daughter who died young, and a son who had to be sent off to America because of some indiscretion or wrongdoing. Despite her writing, she was in financial distress for much of her life and died penniless.

#### DENISE LEVERTOV (b.1923)

Born in Ilford, Essex. She is the younger of two daughters of a Welsh mother and a Russian Jewish father who became a Church of England clergyman. Levertov was educated mainly by her mother, with the addition of some BBC Schools programmes, and private tuition in French, art and music. She was a nurse in World War II, married in 1947 and emigrated to the United States in 1948. She gained US citizenship in 1955. She was active in political campaigns against the Vietnam War, a commitment reflected in her poetry at the time. She has taught at universities in New York, California and Massachusetts. Her first book of poetry was *The Double Image* (1946). Since then, she has published numerous collections and has won a number of awards for her work. *Collected Earlier Poems 1940-1960* appeared in 1979, *Poems 1960-1967* in 1983 and *Selected Poems* in 1986.

#### AMY LEVY (1861-89)

English novelist and poet. Born in Clapham, London. Her father was an editor. She was the first Jewish woman to enter Newnham College, Cambridge. Her first book of poetry, *Xantippe and other Verse* (1881), was published when she was still a student. After university, she travelled around Europe, investigating and writing about the experiences of Jewish communities in various countries. In 1884, *A Minor Poet and Other Verse* appeared. A third volume of poems, *A London Plane Tree*, was published in 1889; the same year, Levy committed suicide by suffocating herself with charcoal fumes.

#### LADY ANNE LINDSAY (1750-1825)

Scottish writer who became famous for one poem, 'Auld Robin Gray', quoted in this book. Daughter of the Earl of Balcarres, she was brought up in Fife, with visits to Edinburgh where her mother and sisters had settled after her father's death in 1768. She was acquainted with the intelligentsia of Edinburgh and met Dr Johnson at the end of his tour of Scotland. In 1770, when her sister left for England to marry a wealthy banker, she felt lonely and sad and tried to lift her spirits 'by attempting a few poetical trifles', of which 'Auld Robin Gray' was one. It was originally published anonymously and became hugely popular.

#### LIZ LOCHHEAD (B.1947)

Scottish poet, dramatist and reviewer. Born in Motherwell. She studied at Glasgow School of Art, and worked as an art teacher for eight years before committing herself to writing full time. *Dreaming Frankenstein and Collected Poems* (1984) and *True Confessions and New Clichés* (1985) contain a good selection of her poetry. She has also done work for television and radio.

#### MARION LOMAX (b.1953)

English poet. Born in Newcastle, she grew up in Northumberland and now lives in Berkshire. Her *Stage Images and Traditions: Shakespeare to Ford* was published in 1987 by Cambridge University Press. In 1981 she won two awards for her poetry; she was Creative Writing Fellow at Reading University 1987-88 and has lectured in English at St Mary's College, Strawberry Hill since 1987. Her first book of poems, *The Peepshow Girl*, was published in 1989.

#### AMY LOWELL (1874-1925)

American poet and critic. Born in Brookline, Massachusetts, into a distinguished New England family. She was a tireless campaigner for poetry. In 1913 she met members of the Imagist movement in London and subsequently (1915-17) published three Imagist anthologies in America. She produced eight collections of her own poetry, three of which were published posthumously, including *What's O'Clock* (1925) which won a Pulitzer Prize. Her biography of John Keats was a standard work for many years. Her contemporaries were said to have been shocked by her cigar-smoking, but even more worried by her free verse.

### GWENDOLYN MACEWEN (1941-87)

Canadian poet, novelist, dramatist and writer for children. Born in Toronto, and educated there and in Winnipeg, leaving school at 18 with the intention of becoming a writer. Shortly after this, she edited a small magazine called *Moment*, and married a Canadian poet, Milton Acorn. In 1963, her first substantial book of poetry was published. She was married briefly to a Greek singer, Nikos Tsingos, and travelled extensively in Israel, Egypt and Greece. Over her short working life, she produced numerous books of poetry and received both the Governor General's Award and the A.J.M. Smith Poetry Prize. Her books of poetry include: *Selah* (1961), *The Drunken Clock* (1961), *The Rising Fire* (1963), *A Breakfast for Barbarians* (1966), *The Shadow Maker* (1969), *The Armies of the Moon* (1972), *Magic Animals* (1975), *The Fire-Eaters* (1976), *The T.E. Lawrence Poems* (1982), *Earthlight* (1982) and *Afterworlds* (1987).

### PHYLLIS MCGINLEY (1905-78)

Born in Ontario, Oregon. She was a teacher in New Rochelle, New York, and wrote poetry when she was not working. She subsequently gave up her teaching post to edit the poetry section of *Town and Country*. She published at least six volumes of poetry, before winning the Pulitzer Prize for Poetry with her *Collected Poetry* (1961).

### SARAH MAGUIRE (b.1957)

English poet, born in London. She left school early, trained as a gardener, and then read English at the University of East Anglia. She now lives in London. Her book *Spilt Milk* was published in 1991.

### MARY DE LA RIVIERE MANLEY (1663-1724)

English novelist, journalist, playwright. Her father was Sir Roger Manley, Lieutenant Governor of Jersey and a Stuart sympathiser. Her Walloon mother died when she was a child, her father when she was about fifteen; she appears to have been left in the care of her cousin John Manley, who later married her under false pretences (he was already married) and left her with a son, a humiliation which severely damaged her social reputation. She became companion to the Duchess of Cleveland, but the two soon quarrelled, and Manley retired to Exeter where she began writing. By 1796 she was in London again and had written two plays, both put on by Sir Thomas Skipwith, manager of the Drury Lane theatre, with whom she is said to have had an affair. After writing two more plays, she began to concentrate on producing scandalous *romans a clef*; as a result of the contents of one of these, she, the printer and publisher were all charged with publishing a scandalous work, but the charges were dropped when Manley refused to name her sources. She produced a number of political pamphlets in support of the Tory faction, established a periodical, *The Female Tatler*, and, in the last ten years of her life published *The Power of Love, in Seven Novels* (1720).

KATHERINE MANSFIELD (1888-1923)
New Zealander; short story writer, poet, critic. Her father was a successful banker in Wellington, New Zealand. In 1903, Mansfield and her older sisters were sent to Queen's College, London. She returned to New Zealand at her parents' insistence in 1906; her first stories were published in 1907. She returned to London in 1908. After a love affair with a violinist, Garret Trowell, she married G.C. Bawden in March 1909 after knowing him for only a few weeks. She left him on the evening of their marriage. Pregnant by Trowell, she went to Germany, where she had a miscarriage; she returned to London in 1910. In 1912, she became involved with John Middleton Murry, and they married in 1918. In 1915, her brother Leslie, to whom she was extremely attached, was killed at the Front. When Mansfield went to the south of France with her husband to recover from her grief, she already had tuberculosis. She spent her remaining eight years wandering round Europe, often in search of a cure. In October 1922, drawn by the teachings of the Russian mystic Gurdjieff, who promised that he could restore her health, she went to Paris. By January the following year she was dead.

'MARNIA' (1968-92)
English poet, short story writer, singer, performer. Born and lived in London. When she was three years old, her father killed her mother. He was in prison for six years during which his daughter grew up in institutions; on his release, 'Marnia' was returned to his care. Almost immediately she began to suffer systematic sexual abuse at the hands of her father and three brothers. Another brother, the one member of the family with whom she had a positive relationship, was murdered in a knife attack when she was seventeen, which provoked her first attempt to kill herself. The remaining five years of her life were to be punctuated by further suicide attempts at points when desperation overwhelmed her. She finally ended her life after having an abortion, to which she had felt driven when she discovered that the baby was male. 'Marnia' began writing in her early teens, at first in diaries, and subsequently produced a considerable body of work consisting of short stories and poetry. The poems in this collection are published for the first time.

FLORENCE RIPLEY MASTIN (late 19th/early 20th century)
American poet. The poem included in this anthology appeared in *Poetry: A Magazine of Verse* in August 1922.

GERDA MAYER (b.1927)
English poet. Born in Czechoslovakia, she now lives in London. Her books include: *Monkey on the Analyst's Couch* (1980), *The Candy Floss Tree* (1984) and *March Postman* (1985).

CHARLOTTE MEW (1869-1928)
English poet and short story writer; born in London. Her father was an architect. She was the third of seven children who seem to have been peculiarly ill-starred: two died in infancy; a third died aged five; two more became

insane and were sent to asylums. Unsurprisingly, Charlotte formed a strong attachment to her remaining sister Anne. She attended a girls' school in Gower Street, then lectures at University College. Her first collection of poetry, *The Farmer's Bride*, appeared in 1916, courtesy of Harold Munro's Poetry Bookshop, but it sold badly. Her second collection, *The Rambling Sailor* (1929), was published posthumously. Mew lived under great financial and psychological strain – two children in private hospitals was an expensive commitment for the family – and suffered enduring guilt from watching Anne fail to receive any recognition for her artistic endeavours, whilst her own work was admired. She never married, explaining to a friend that she and Anne did not want to risk passing on any hereditary mental illness. However, it seems that she did fall in love with May Sinclair (an influential figure in the English literary world at the time); her passion was entirely unrequited and at first bewildered Sinclair, then earned her scorn. Mew's mother died in 1923, and her sister Anne died of cancer in 1927. Early in 1928 Charlotte Mew was admitted to hospital, where neurasthenia was diagnosed. In March of that year, she killed herself by drinking Lysol. Her *Collected Poems* was published in 1953.

### ALICE MEYNELL (1847-1922)

English poet and essayist. Her mother, Christina Weller, was a concert pianist. Meynell and her sister were educated primarily by their father, James Thompson, a Cambridge graduate and writer. The family lived a Bohemian life in France, England, Italy and Switzerland during Meynell's early years before returning to a more conventional life. At the age of twenty, she was converted to Roman Catholicism. Her first volume of poetry, *Preludes*, published in 1875, was well received; she wrote seven further books of poetry and twelve of essays. In 1877 she married Wilfred Meynell, a Catholic journalist, and the couple had eight children. She supported women's suffrage (though not militancy), and during World War I became drawn to pacifism. Her work was highly regarded by the Victorian literary establishment. *The Poems of Alice Meynell* was published in 1940.

### VIOLA MEYNELL (1888-1956)

English poet whose work was published in magazines and journals.

### SUSAN MILES (late 19th/early 20th century)

English poet.

### EDNA ST VINCENT MILLAY (1892-1950)

American poet and dramatist. She was born in Rockland, Maine; the eldest of three daughters, her father was a schoolteacher and school superintendent who left the family when Millay was seven. Her mother, a nurse, made considerable efforts to encourage her children in artistic pursuits. A poem called 'Renascence', published in an anthology in 1912, led to the opportunity for Millay to go to Vassar College. In 1917 she moved to Greenwich Village. She won the Pulitzer Prize for Poetry for *The Harp Weaver and other Poems* (1923), and published at least ten books of verse. Her popularity was at its height in the 1920s. She was married to a Dutch businessman for 27 years until his death in 1949. In his later years, he gave up his coffee business to help in the organisation of Millay's highly successful poetry reading tours and to manage their farm, Steepletop, in Upstate New York. Her *Collected Poems* was published in 1956.

RUTH MILLER (1919-69)
South African poet. She was born in Cape Province. One book of poetry, *Floating Island*, was published in 1965, and a volume of selected poetry appeared in 1968.

SUSANNA VALENTINE MITCHELL (early 20th century)
American poet. The poem in this book was found in a 1935 anthology of verse first published in American journals and magazines at the beginning of this century.

NAOMI MITCHISON (b.1897)
Scottish novelist, journalist, polemicist, writer for children and poet. Born in Edinburgh, she was brought up in Oxford, though summers were spent on the family estate in Auchterarder. Her father was the psychologist, J.S. Haldane. In 1916 she married a Labour politician. In the 1960s, she lived in Africa, where she developed a particular interest in the Bakgatha tribe of Botswana; they adopted her as their adviser and 'mother' (Mmarona). She is best known for her novels. Her books of poetry include: *The Delicate Fire* (1933) and *The Cleansing of the Knife* (1978).

MARY MONK (?1677-1715)
Little is known of the second daughter of Robert, First Viscount Molesworth except that she married George Monk of Dublin and died at Bath of a 'languishing sickness'. A year after her death, her father published a collection of her work under the title, *Marinda: Poems and Translations Upon Several Occasions*.

LADY MARY WORTLEY MONTAGU (1689-1762)
English poet and letter writer. Born in London, the daughter of Evelyn Pierrepont, Earl of Kingston (and later Duke of Kingston). Her mother died when she was a child. She read widely as a young woman and learnt both Latin and Greek. In 1712, she married Edward Wortley Montagu (a politician) against her father's wishes (he had ordered her to marry another man). In 1715, she contracted smallpox which wrecked her looks, leaving her with damaged skin and no eyelashes. She accompanied her husband on an official trip to Constantinople (1716-18) and, on her return to England, introduced inoculation for smallpox, which she had seen practised in Turkey. She was greatly criticised for having her own two children inoculated. She was prominent in London society and appeared at Court; she knew and corresponded with Alexander Pope, though he later turned on her, possibly because she had repudiated his advances. Her relationship with her husband did not flourish. She wrote verses and a political periodical. In 1736, infatuated by a twenty-four-year-old Italian bisexual, she travelled round Europe in his wake, but failed to awaken his interest. She lived abroad for the next twenty years, finally returning to England when her husband died in 1761. Her most famous writings are her *Letters*, some of which were published in 1763.

MRS B-LL M-RT-N (fl.1726)
English poet. Her identity remains entirely obscure. The poem in this collection
comes from *A New Miscellany . . . Written Chiefly by Persons of Quality* (c.1726).

EDITH NESBIT (1858-1924)
English writer for children, novelist and poet. Youngest of four surviving
children of the head of an agricultural college. Her father died when she
was four. Part of her childhood was spent in France and Germany where
the family had moved for the health of a tubercular sister, who died in
1871, after which they returned to England. At about 15 Nesbit began to
publish verse in magazines. In 1880 she married Hubert Bland, a partner in
a small brush-making business. Shortly after, Bland contracted smallpox,
and his partner in business disappeared with all the company's funds, leaving
the family penniless. Edith Nesbit now had to support her family by her
writing activities, as well as two other children fathered by her husband,
who was something of a philanderer. She and her husband were founding
members of the Fabian Society, and it was through the society's meetings
that she met and fell in love with George Bernard Shaw, but nothing came
of this. Her youngest son died tragically under anaesthetic; she lost her
husband four years later. In 1917 she remarried and moved to the Kent
coast. She was best known for her children's books, which included *The
Wouldbegoods* (1901) and *The Railway Children* (1906).

GRACE NICHOLS (b.1950)
British Guyanese. Poet, novelist, short story writer, journalist. Born in
Georgetown, Guyana. She came to Britain in 1977. Her first book of poems
for adults, *i is a long memoried woman*, won the 1983 Commonweath Poetry
Prize. Since then she has published *The Fat Black Woman's Poems* - which
includes her first book together with a collection called *Back Home From
Contemplation* – (1985) and *Lazy Thoughts of a Lazy Woman* (1989). She lives in
Sussex with her husband, the poet John Agard, and their daughter.

SHARON OLDS
American poet. She teaches at New York University and at Goldwater Hos-
pital, Roosevelt Island, New York. Her books include *Satan Says* (1980), *The
Dead and the Living* (1984) and *The Gold Cell* (1987).

ROSE O'NEILL (late 19th/early 20th century)
American poet. Published in magazines and journals in the 1920s and 1930s.

DOROTHY PARKER (1893-1967)
American wit and poet. She was the only daughter of a Jewish father and
Scottish mother, who died while she was still a small child. At 23, she worked
in a minor editorial capacity for *Vogue*, and within a year she was drama
critic for *Vanity Fair*. In 1917, she married Edward Pond Parker; the couple
divorced in 1928. Celebrated for her sharp and witty pronouncements, she
belonged to the fashionable literary clique, the Algonquin Round Table.
Her first volume of poetry, *Enough Rope* (1926), was a bestseller; it was followed
by *Sunset Gun* (1928), *Death and Taxes* (1931) and *Not So Deep as a Well* (1936).
She worked with her second husband in Hollywood. After his death, she
took to drink and died alone in a Manhattan hotel room.

### KATHERINE PHILIPS (1631-64)

English poet. Born in London, the daughter of a merchant. A cousin provided much of her early education, which was completed at a fashionable boarding school. She married James Philips of Cardigan in 1647. She was at the centre of a circle of friendship consisting exclusively of women, to whom many of her poems are addressed. Her admirers knew her as 'The Matchless Orinda'. Some of her best known poems are addressed to 'Lucasia' (Anne Owens). She died of smallpox, at the height of her popularity. Her *Poems* was published in 1667.

### MARGE PIERCY (b.1936)

American novelist and poet. Born in Detroit. Her books of poetry include: *Breaking Camp* (1968), *Hard Loving* (1969), *To Be of Use* (1973), *Living in the Open* (1976), *My Mother's Body, Stone, Paper, Knife* and *Circles on the Water*.

### LAETITIA PILKINGTON (?1708-50)

English poet. Born in Dublin. Her father was a physician of Dutch extraction who had settled in Ireland. Encouraged by her father, she read and wrote poetry from an early age. She married a poet and clergyman, Matthew Pilkington. Through one of her friends, the couple was introduced to the literary circle around Jonathan Swift, which included Mary Barber. Matthew Pilkington moved to London, and by the time his wife followed him there, having left their three children with her parents, he was already involved in an affair with an actress. She returned alone to Dublin. In 1738, her husband obtained a divorce from her on grounds of her adultery, something which she denied but which did great damage to her reputation. She moved back to London, leaving her children with her husband. She made attempts to collect subscriptions which would enable her to publish her poems, but they never appeared. In 1742, she was imprisoned for debt; Colley Cibber came to her rescue. She knew and corresponded with the novelist Samuel Richardson. For a short time she had a pamphlet and print shop in St James's Street, but various personal problems and a burglary befell her, and in 1747 she returned to Dublin, where the first volume of her *Memoirs* was published. Within days of her death in 1750, her husband had remarried; he later disowned their children in his will.

### SYLVIA PLATH (1932-63)

American poet born in Boston. Her father was a German émigré from Poland who became a biologist at Boston University; her mother, also a German immigrant, was a high-school English teacher. Plath demonstrated a precocious talent for writing and drawing. Her father died when she was eight. By the time she was at Smith College, she had had drawings, poems and stories published in national magazines and journals. She graduated in 1955, also winning awards for her poetry. She won a Fulbright scholarship to Cambridge, where she met and married the poet, Ted Hughes. She returned briefly to Smith as an English professor, but a year later decided to move back to England. She had two children and the strains of bringing them up, coping with chronic ill health and depression and facing difficulties in her marriage while trying to write took a heavy toll: she committed suicide at the age of 31. Her books of poetry are *The Colossus* (1960), *Ariel* (1965), *Crossing the Water* (1971) and *Winter Trees*. Her *Collected Poems* was published in 1981.

British/Trinidadian poet. She was born in Trinidad but in the 1950s came to England, where she now lives and works. Her first collection of poetry, *Land of Rope and Tory*, was published in 1985.

KATHLEEN RAINE (b.1908)
English poet, literary critic, translator, and autobiographer. Her father, an English teacher at the County High School in Ilford, Essex, was also a Methodist preacher and an active pacifist; her mother, a Scot, had an enduring influence on her daughter. She spent much of her childhood in Northumberland with her maternal grandmother. Raine read natural sciences at Girton College, Cambridge. Her first volume of poetry, *Stone and Flower*, appeared in 1943. She has received many awards for her work. Her *Collected Poems* appeared in 1956, since when she has published several further books of poetry.

ADRIENNE RICH (b.1929)
American poet and essayist. Brought up in a Jewish household in Baltimore, Maryland. Initially educated by her father and mother (a professor of medicine and a trained composer and pianist), who encouraged her to read and write, she had a wide knowledge of the great eighteenth- and nineteenth-century English poets at an early age. Rich wrote her first poetry as a child. She attended Radcliffe College and graduated in 1951; her first book of poems, *A Change of World*, was published in the same year. She married and had three sons; her husband died in 1978. She continued in her professorship at Rutgers University in New York until 1979 when she settled in Massachusetts 'with the woman who shares my life'. She is well known as a writer on lesbian feminist issues. Her books of poetry include: *The Diamond Cutters* (1955), *Snapshots of a Daughter in Law* (1963), *Leaflets: Poems 1965-1968* (1969), *The Will to Change* (1971), *Diving into the Wreck* (1973) – for which she won the 1974 National Book Award for poetry – , *Dream of a Common Language: Poems 1974-77* (1978), *A Wild Patience Has Taken Me This Far* (1981), *The Fact of a Doorframe: Poems Selected and New 1954-1984* (1984), *Your Native Land/Your Life* (1986).

MAIMIE A. RICHARDSON (fl.1920s)
Scottish poet. Author of *Moods and Dreams* (1926), *The Song of Gold* (1928) and *Poems* (1931).

ELIZABETH RIDDELL (b.1910)
Australian poet and journalist. Born in New Zealand. She settled in Australia soon after leaving school. One of Australia's most successful journalists, she was a correspondent in London during World War II and has also worked in the United States. She was married to the journalist E.N. Greatorex. She has published four books of poetry.

ANNE RIDLER (b.1912)
English poet and dramatist. Born at Rugby. Her father and uncle were housemasters at Rugby School. She married in 1938 and has two daughters and a son. Her books include *Poems* (1939), *The Nine Bright Shiners* (1943), *The Golden Bird and other poems* (1951), *A Matter of Life and Death* (1959), *Some Time After* (1973).

CORINNE ROOSEVELT ROBINSON (late 19th/early 20th century)
American poet. The poem in this book is taken from an anthology of poetry compiled by Sara Teasdale and published in 1917.

CHRISTINA ROSSETTI (1830-94)
English poet, writer for children and artist. Born in London. Her father was a political refugee from Naples; her mother was also of Italian descent. Rossetti was educated at home and her first books of poetry were privately printed when she was twelve and seventeen. After her father retired from his post as professor of Italian at the University of London because of ill health, she supplemented the family's income by teaching Italian and writing, in the course of which she met and fell in love with Charles Cayley (among his achievements was translating the Bible into Iroquois Indian). She remained devoted to him for the rest of her life, though the couple never married. For some time, Rossetti did charity work at a refuge for single mothers and prostitutes in Highgate. In 1862, her first collection of poetry, *Goblin Market and Other Poems*, came out. She became a prolific poet. In 1865 she was incorrectly diagnosed as having contracted tuberculosis, and became increasingly ill. In 1871 her complaint was finally correctly identified as Graves Disease, the symptoms of which were bulging eyes, darkening of the skin, loss of hair and heart attacks. Over the next ten years, becoming increasingly infirm, she developed an obsession about death, which is reflected in much of her verse. Her sister Maria died of cancer in 1881, and the deaths of her brother Dante Gabriel and her beloved Charles Cayley followed two years later. She survived for another ten years.

ELIZABETH SINGER ROWE (1674-1737)
English poet, translator, writer of devotional works and epistolary fiction. The eldest of three daughters of a clothier and Dissenting preacher and an extremely pious woman who met her husband in the course of visiting prisoners. Rowe was educated at a country boarding school. Her mother died when she was 16 but she was close to her father, who gave her instruction in religion, art, music and literature. Her *Poems on Several Occasions* (1696), published under the name of Philomela, was immediately successful and she became widely known as 'the Heavenly Singer'. In 1710, she married Thomas Rowe, a poet and scholar thirteen years her junior with whom she had fallen deeply in love. Their union was brought to an abrupt end five years later by Thomas's death from tuberculosis. Rowe returned to her father's home and died at 62, apparently of apoplexy.

CAROL RUMENS (b.1944)
English poet and novelist. She lives in London and has two children. An erstwhile poetry editor for *Literary Review*, she is a Fellow of the Royal Society of Literature. Her books of poetry include *Unplayed Music* (1981), *Star Whisper* (1983), *Direct Dialling* (1985) and *The Greening of the Snow Beach* (1988).

MARTHA SANSOM (1690-1736)
English poet, born in Herefordshire. She was educated by her mother as a Roman Catholic, learned French and started writing at an early age. In 1708, her father was murdered (to which she refers in her writings). As a young woman, she spent part of her time in fashionable circles in London

and part in rural Fulham. In 1720, *Epistles of Clio and Strephon* was published, an exchange in verse with the writer William Bond. She was part of the literary circle that surrounded the poet and playwright Aaron Hill, and is said to have fallen madly in love with him. Her literary name, by which she was well known, was Clio. A number of her poems appeared in *New Miscellany* (1720). By 1726 she had married Arnold Sansom, a wealthy lawyer, and the couple retired to Leicestershire. Her autobiographical *Clio, or a Secret History of the Life and Amours of the Late celebrated Mrs S–N–M*, published in 1752 (probably after being found among the papers of Aaron Hill, who died in 1750), contained many passionate poems addressed to Hill.

### MARY SAVAGE (fl.1763-77)
English poet whose identity remains obscure. Her two volumes of *Poems on Various Subjects and Occasions* (1777) are prefaced by a 'Letter to Miss E.B.' in which the author claims that she has had no education, refers to experiencing 'cares of the world' and alludes to being forced to stay at home rather than being free to socialise – 'I have the care of a large Family which really finds me full employment'.

### ANNA SAWYER (fl.1794-1801)
English poet. Roger Lonsdale (editor of *The Oxford Book Eighteenth Century Women Poets*, 1989) has deduced from her *Poems on Various Subjects* that she lived at one time near Rowberrow, not far from Cheddar in Somerset; also that some mishap befell her husband which forced the couple to move to Birmingham. It appears that her friends encouraged her to publish her poems 'in the fond hope of dispersing the clouds that hovered over her worthy Husband in his declining years'. Subscribers to the publication included the religious writer Hannah More (1745-1833) and the poet Anna Seward (1747-1809).

### LADY JOHN SCOTT (1810-1900)
Scottish poet (Alicia Anne Spottiswood of that ilk) whose life remains obscure.

### ANNE SEXTON (1928-74)
American poet, born in Newton, Massachusetts. For most of her life she lived in Weston. She married Alfred Sexton on an impulse in 1948 and the marriage was difficult; it finally ended in divorce in 1973. As a result of attacks of suicidal depression, Sexton was separated from her two young daughters. Her first book, *To Bedlam and Part Way Back*, was published in 1960; she won the Pulitzer Prize for *Live or Die* (1967). She taught for some years at Boston University before committing suicide at the age of 46. Her *Complete Poems* was published in 1981.

### MARY WOLLSTONECRAFT SHELLEY (1797-1851)
English novelist, biographer and poet. She was the only child of William Godwin and Mary Wollstonecraft (both prominent radical writers). Her mother died ten days after Mary's birth, and she grew up in the company of a stepbrother and stepsister. In 1814, much to her father's disapproval, she began a relationship with his friend Percy Bysshe Shelley who had visited the house with his wife Harriet, and a few months later the two went on a trip to continental Europe, an action which led to her father refusing to communicate with her. In 1816, having lost one premature baby, she bore a

son, William. In the summer of that year, the family went to Lake Geneva where they spent much time with Byron, and Mary began the novel which was to become a bestseller, *Frankenstein*. Harriet Shelley was found drowned in the Serpentine (an ornamental lake in London) in December 1816, and the couple married immediately. Their daughter Clare was born in 1817. In 1818 *Frankenstein* was published anonymously; it was some years before the public realised that its author was a young woman. The Shelleys returned to Italy, but within months of their arrival their two children were dead. In 1819 another son, Percy Florence, was born, but his father died the following year. Mary Shelley devoted her remaining years to nurturing her remaining child, and lived to see him happily married.

PENELOPE SHUTTLE (b.1947)
English poet and novelist. She has lived in Cornwall since 1970 when she moved there to live with the poet Peter Redgrove. They married in 1980 and have a daughter. The two writers have collaborated on several novels and books of poetry, but their major work together is a psychological study of menstruation, *The Wise Wound*. Shuttle has won a number of awards for her work. Her books of poetry include: *The Orchard Upstairs* (1980), *The Child-Stealer* (1983) and *Adventures with my Horse* (1988).

ELIZABETH SIDDAL (1834-62)
English artist and poet. Daughter of a London cutler, she probably worked in a milliner's shop. After being discovered by the artist Walter Deverell (1827-54), she sat as a model for the Pre-Raphaelite circle. Soon, she began to paint on her own account, roundly encouraged by Ruskin, who bought 'every scrap of her designs'. She married Dante Gabriel Rossetti in 1860, but it was by then not a happy relationship.. After a long illness, she died of an overdose of laudanum.

EDITH SITWELL (1887-1964)
English poet, critic and novelist. The eldest of three children of Sir George and Lady Sitwell of Renishaw Hall. Her mother was a young spendthrift beauty; her father became ever more self-centred and eccentric as he grew older, devoting himself more or less exclusively to research into his ancestry, and preoccupied by his illnesses. Unlike her brothers Osbert and Sacheverell, she was educated at home by governesses. Not conventionally attractive or ladylike, she immersed herself in poetry and music. When she was 16, a governess was engaged who shared her love of French poetry, and at 27, when she became financially independent, the two moved into a flat in Bayswater, London. Her financial position was always precarious (before World War II she often stayed in Paris where life was cheaper), and she suffered repeatedly from illness all her life. She became notorious for self-advertisement, often adopting Elizabethan dress, and holding eccentric opinions which she readily expressed. Perhaps best known for *Façade* (1923), verse set to music by Sir William Walton. Her *Collected Poems* was published in 1957.

STEVIE SMITH (1902-71)
English poet and novelist. At three, she moved with her mother from Yorkshire to Palmer's Green in London; her father had gone to sea shortly before she was born and never returned. When her mother died, Smith's

aunt moved in and the two became lifelong companions until her aunt's death in 1968. Smith worked as a publisher's secretary, 1923-53. When she took her first collection of poems to the publisher Jonathan Cape, she was advised to go away and write a novel, which she did (*Novel on Yellow Paper*, 1936). The first of her nine books of poetry, *A Good Time Was Had By All*, was published in 1937. She won the Cholmondeley Award in 1966 and the Queen's Medal for Poetry in 1969. She regularly recited and sang her poems in public readings and on radio. Her *Collected Poems* was published in 1975.

#### KATHLEEN SPIVACK (b.1938)
American poet. Her poems have appeared in numerous magazines. Her books include: *Flying Inland* (1973) and *The Jane Poems* (1974).

#### MARGARET STANLEY-WRENCH (b.1916)
English poet and journalist. She attended Somerville College, Oxford. In 1937, she won the Newdigate Prize for *The Man in the Moon*. Her books include: *Newsreel and Other Poems* (1938), *The Splendid Burden* (a verse play) and *A Tale for the Fall of the Year* (1959).

#### ANNE STEVENSON (b.1933)
American poet and critic. Born in Cambridge (England) of American parents, while her father was studying there. She spent her childhood in Vermont, but has spent most of her adult life in England and has now settled in Durham, where she lives with her husband. She began writing when she was a student at the University of Michigan. Her seven books of poetry include *Living in America* (1965), *Reversals* (1969), *Enough of Green* (1977), *Minute by Glass Minute* (1982), *The Fiction Makers* (1985); her *Selected Poems* (1956-86) was published in 1987. She has also written a biography of Sylvia Plath.

#### MARION STROBEL (fl.1920s)
American poet. The poem in this collection was found in *Poetry: A Magazine of Verse*, Chicago, March 1923.

#### JAN STRUTHER (1901-53)
Actually J. Anstruther. English novelist, essayist, poet. She was married first to the senior partner of an Edinburgh law firm, then, following her move to the United States with two of her three children, to a librarian at Columbia University. She was known almost exclusively for 'Mrs Miniver's Diary', a popular column in *The Times*, which described English middle-class family life before World War II; she then published a book *Mrs Miniver* (1939), which became a huge best-seller and was subsquently made into a film. So exasperated did she become at being identified solely with this book, that when a contest was organised for the best parody of it, she submitted a biting entry under a pen name, won the competition and handed the prize money to an organisation for distressed gentlewomen.

#### MURIEL STUART (d.1967)
English poet, journalist and dramatist. She was born in the countryside just outside London; her father was a member of the West Country gentry; her mother came from Scotland. She worked as a Fleet Street journalist for many years. Her books of poetry include: *The Cockpit of Idols* (1918), *Poems* (1922) and *Selected Poems* (1927).

MAY SWENSON (b.1919)
American journalist and poet. Born into a large Mormon family, she grew up and was educated near the State University in Logan, Utah, where her father was professor of mechanical engineering. After attending university, she worked as a reporter on a newspaper in Salt Lake City. Later she moved to New York, where, among other occupations, she was editor of *New Directions* in 1959. From 1966 she devoted herself full time to writing. She received numerous awards for her poetry. Her books include *To Mix With Time: New and Selected Poems* (1963) and *New and Selected Things Taking Place* (1978).

ELIZABETH TAYLOR (fl.c.1685-1720)
English poet. *Kissing the Rod* (ed. Greer, Medoff, Sanson & Hastings, 1988) identifies her as the wife of a judge, Sir Francis Wythens (?1634-1704), and the Mrs Taylor who contributed three songs to the *Miscellany* put together by Aphra Behn, of which the poem in this collection is one. Lady Wythens moved out of her husband's house soon after they married and made her home near the country residence of Sir Thomas Colepepper, third and last baronet of Preston Hall, Aylesford. Unable or unwilling to accept that she had a lover, her husband continued to visit her; Lady Wythens finally moved to Colepepper's villa, and Wythens was sued by Colepepper for financial support for the children she had brought with her. Wythens died in 1704, leaving his widow free to marry Colepepper.

SARA TEASDALE (1884-1933)
American poet. Born into a wealthy family, the youngest of four children. She was educated at home until the age of nine, apparently because of an excessively nervous temperament, but later had a more formal education. After graduating, she and some friends published a magazine in which many of her early poems appeared. She developed a romantic liaison with the poet Vachel Lindsay, and then with a St Louis businessman called Ernst Filsinger whom she married in 1914. But her devotion to poetry created tensions in the marriage, and it was dissolved in 1929. There followed for Teasdale four years of worsening health and intense depression, and in 1933, fearful, it is said, that she would become a helpless invalid, she killed herself by taking an overdose. Her books include: *Sonnets to Duse* (1907), *Rivers to the Sea, Flame and Shadow* (1920), *Love Songs* (1928), *Dark of the Moon* (1930) and *Strange Victory* (1933).

LILY THICKNESSE (fl. early 20th century)
English poet. The poem included in this collection comes from *Poems Old and New* (London, 1909).

ELIZABETH THOMAS (1675-1731)
English poet. Her father, a member of the Inner Temple, was 42 years older than his wife; he died when his daughter was two. Thomas educated herself by reading, and by her mid-twenties was writing poetry, some of which she showed to the poet John Dryden and other literary figures. She corresponded with other female poets, particularly respecting Lady Chudleigh for her *The Ladies Defence*. She received several offers of marriage, notably from Richard Gwinnet, a lawyer who wrote in his free time and whom she had met in a bookshop. He finally proposed to her in 1716, when he had come into an

inheritance, but by then she was committed to nursing her invalid mother, and was not immediately able to accept his offer. He died a few months later and she was forced to litigate with his family for eight years to obtain only £213 of the £600 he had left to her. The next years were poverty-stricken and miserable for her. Having avoided publication of her work for many years, she finally published her *Miscellany Poems* in 1722; she also sold various letters from literary figures like Pope, Dryden and Lady Chudleigh, but she was unable to hold her creditors at bay and 1727 found her in Fleet Prison. She was released in 1729, published *The Metamorphosis of the Town: or a View of the Present Fashions* in 1730, and died in 1731.

ELIZABETH TOLLET (1694-1754)
English poet. Daughter of George Tollet, a Commissioner of the Navy, who, encouraged by his friend Sir Isaac Newton, gave her an excellent education. Her *Poems on Several Occasions* was published anonymously in 1724. Another volume, *Poems*, published in her name, appeared the year after her death, omitting some of the poems that had been in the first book, and adding new ones.

ROSEMARY TONKS (b.1932)
English poet and novelist. She has published two books of poetry and seven novels.

ELIZABETH TREFUSIS (fl. early 19th century)
English poet.

ESTHER VANHOMRIGH (early 18th century)
English poet who wrote under the name, 'Vanessa'.

JUDITH VIORST
American poet. She is married to the political writer Milton Viorst and has three sons. Her books include: *It's Hard to Be Hip Over Thirty and Other Tragedies of Married Life* (1968) and *People and Other Aggravations* (1969).

EDA LOU WALTON (fl.1920s)
American poet. The verse in this collection is an extract taken from a poem published in *Poetry: A Magazine of Verse*, Chicago, August 1921.

MAY THIELGAARD WATTS (fl.1920s)
American poet whose verse appeared in literary journals.

MARY GLADYS WEBB (1881-1927)
English poet, novelist, essayist and short story writer. Born in Shropshire, she was the eldest of six children; her father was head of a boarding school in Leighton. She was educated chiefly at home. She began writing verse at the age of ten. When she was about fourteen her mother was injured in a hunting accident, and for five years Mary Webb was responsible for running the household. Soon after her twentieth birthday, it was discovered that she had Graves Disease. Her father's death in 1909 affected her deeply. In 1910 she met Henry Webb, a school teacher, and in 1912 the couple married; guests at their wedding included seventy women inmates from the local workhouse. In 1924 she was awarded the Femina Vie Heureuse Prize for *Precious Bane*, the book for which she was chiefly known. Her last two years

were unhappy: both her health and her marriage were failing. Her *Poems* was published in 1928.

## ANNE WHARTON (?1659-85)

English poet and dramatist. Her father, Sir Henry Lee, died of the plague several months before she was born; her mother died in childbirth. She (and her sister) inherited extensive properties in Oxfordshire and near London. Her grandmother brought her up, but at the age of twelve she was already the subject of marriage plans, and in 1673, in accordance with the political ambitions of her guardian, Sir Ralph Verney, she was married to Thomas Wharton, who later became the Whigs' leader in Parliament. Wharton was plainly more attracted to his wife's dowry than to her, and she was frequently lonely and ill, though remained devoted to him. She corresponded with many literary figures of the time, among them Edmund Waller, Aphra Behn and Robert Wolseley. A number of poets addressed poems to her. After her death, her will, which left everything to her husband, was vigorously contested by her grandmother, who claimed that her granddaughter had been given the pox by her husband and then deserted by him. Her poems were published in a number of anthologies after her death, and more appeared in *Whartoniana* in 1727.

## EDITH NEWBOLD WHARTON (1862-1937)

American novelist and poet. She was born into an old New York family: she could trace both sides of her family back 300 years. She was educated by governesses, travelled widely in Europe and then married a Bostonian, Edward Wharton, in 1885. The couple had extremely different temperaments, and their marriage proved difficult. Edith Wharton suffered a series of nervous breakdowns from 1898 to 1902; her husband had a breakdown in 1907, and the couple divorced in 1913. At about this time, apparently partly as a tonic, Wharton started writing. She had already established a home for herself in France, and during World War I, she was centrally involved in an organisation set up to aid refugees; in 1916 the French government awarded her the Légion d'Honneur. Apart from one short trip to the United States in 1923, she remained in France. She was mainly known for her novels; her *Verses* was privately printed in 1878.

## ANNA WICKHAM (1884-1947)

English poet. She was born Edith Alice Mary Harper. Her father was a piano tuner with artistic ambitions; her mother a flamboyant figure who taught elocution, and practised hypnotism and professional character reading. Much of her childhood was spent in Australia. She adopted her pen name before she was in her teens; it derived from an address, Wickham Terrace, Brisbane, where, when she was ten, her father had assured her that she would one day be a poet. She began writing verse at six, and produced it compulsively, composing over 1,400 poems in all. For twenty-eight years, none of it was published; for a long time after her marriage, her husband had no idea that she wrote poetry. Her first volume was published under a pseudonym (John Oland) by Harold Munro at the Poetry Bookshop in 1911. Patrick Hepburn, her husband, and his highly conventional family did not appreciate, indeed were embarrassed by her writing. He told her that her work was worthless; she reacted with fury, and found herself promptly certified insane. When she was released from the mental home to which she had been consigned, she returned to her husband out of devotion to her two young sons. In 1929 Hepburn died in a mountaineering accident which bore an eerie resemblance to an episode described in one of Wickham's poems written eight years before. By the 1930s, her reputation as a poet was established.

### ELLA WHEELER WILCOX (1850-1919)

American poet. Born in Wisconsin, she was the youngest of four children of a music teacher who abandoned his profession to become a farmer, and a mother who had strong literary ambitions. At the age of ten she wrote a novel, and by eighteen she was earning a good living from her writing. When she first tried to publish her *Poems of Passion* (1883), many of which had already appeared in various periodicals, the book was rejected by publishers on grounds of immorality, a reaction which undoubtedly contributed to its considerable sales when it was finally published. Other books followed including: *Poems of Pleasure, Poems of Love* and *Poems of Sentiment.* In 1918, she toured army camps in France, giving talks on sexual problems, but as a result of severe fatigue, she fell ill in the spring of 1919 and died.

### SARAH WILLIAMS (1841-68)

English poet. The verse in this collection is an extract from a poem found in her *Twilight Hours* (1868).

### ELIZABETH WILMOT, COUNTESS OF ROCHESTER (d.1681)

English poet. She was brought up in Somerset. As a young woman, she moved to London, and two years later, in 1667, much against her family's wishes, she married the poet John Wilmot, second Earl of Rochester, a prominent member of Charles II's court. She moved to his house in Oxfordshire; the couple had a son who died in infancy and three daughters.

### SHEILA WINGFIELD (1906-92)

English poet. Daughter of Viscount Powerscourt. Her early education was directed by a series of governesses at home in London. Her parents disapproved of her interest in reading and writing poetry. In 1932, she married the Hon. Mervyn Wingfield. In spite of his qualified feelings about her poetic bent (he disliked meeting her literary friends), her first volume, *Poems*, was published in 1938. She coped with a serious illness for over thirty years during which she continued to publish. Towards the end of her life, she lived in Switzerland for many years. Her books include: *Beat Drum, Beat Heart* (1946), *A Cloud Across the Sun* (1949), *A Kite's Dinner* (1954), *The Leaves Darken* (1964), *Her Storms* (1974) and *Admissions* (1977). Her *Collected Poems* was published in 1983.

### JUDITH WRIGHT (b.1915)

Australian poet, essayist, short story writer and writer for children. Born into the fifth generation of a pioneeer farming family at Armidale in northern New South Wales. In 1936 she graduated from Sydney University. She was the first Australian female poet to establish an international reputation. Five Australian universities have awarded her honorary degrees and her work, which is regularly studied in Australian schools and universities, has received numerous awards. She is also well known for her support for nature conservation and for Aboriginal land rights. She has published over ten individual collections of poetry; her *Collected Poems 1942-1970* was published in 1972.

MEHETABEL WRIGHT (1697-1750)

English poet. Known in her family as Hetty, and often referred to by this name in anthologies. The seventh of nineteen children of a Lincolnshire clergyman, Samuel Wesley. She was educated to the same level as her brothers, who included John and Charles Wesley, the founders of Methodism. She came into conflict with her family when she fell in love with a lawyer, of whom her father disapproved, and eloped with him in 1725. She returned later in the year, having entered into a relationship with another man. Almost certainly already pregnant, she was married to William Wright of Louth in October 1725. Her daughter did not reach the age of one. By 1727, the couple had settled in London, where her husband worked as a plumber and glazier in Soho. Her relations with her father remained strained, and she clearly resented that she had been forced into 'wedlock without love'. Roger Lonsdale (*Oxford Book of Eighteenth Century Verse*, 1989) reports that her husband was 'her social and intellectual inferior, who preferred to spend his evenings drinking with "low company" and soon "broke the heart of his wife".' During 1743, she was increasingly influenced by her brother John's Methodism, and in the following year when she convalesced with the Wesley family after a serious illness, she became even more pious. After her death in 1750, some of her poems were circulated in manuscript, and a few subsequently appeared in anthologies. A collected edition of her work was finally published in the nineteenth century.

LADY MARY SIDNEY WROTH (?1586-?1640)

English poet. Daughter of Robert, Earl of Leicester and niece of Sir Philip Sidney and of Mary Herbert, Countess of Pembroke, both poets. She spent her childhood in the Netherlands (where her father was Governor of Flushing) and at Penshurst (in Kent) surrounded by poets and poetry. Negotiations for Lady Mary's marriage started when she was twelve years old; she became the wife of Sir Robert Wroth, son of a wealthy landowner whose interests lay in sport rather than literature. She cultivated a circle of friends and acquaintances among poets; he devoted himself to exploiting his estate to provide James I with good hunting. She bore a son, James, in February 1614. Her husband died a month later, leaving her with an estate beset with debt. When her son died at the age of two and a half, the estate reverted to her husband's family and she spent the rest of her life in financial difficulty, often under siege from creditors. In widowhood it seems that her long-standing love for her cousin William Herbert, third Earl of Pembroke, was finally consummated; there were probably two children, both undoubtedly fostered outside the family. In 1621, *The Countess of Montgomeries Urania* appeared, scandalously for the time, under her own name. She was attacked because of the clear connection between events and people in her own life and the feelings and opinions related in *Urania*. Little is known about the rest of her life except that she needed repeated protection from creditors.

## INDEX OF TITLES

Accoutrement, 193
Advice To Her Son On Marriage, 167
Against Coupling, 107
Ah Me, If I Grew Sweet To Man, 158
Airing the Chapel, 271
And Again, 275
And On My Eyes Dark Sleep By Night, 5
Angellica's Lament, 245
Answer to a Love-Letter, An, 34
Appeal, 213
Art of Coquetry, The (extract from), 40
Aspects of Love (extract from), 81
At A Reception, 112
At Les Deux Magots, 207
At Parting, 229
At Sixteen, 7
At 3 a.m., 45
Attraction, 125
Auld Robin Gray, 26
Auld Robin Forbes, 239
Autumn, 285
Avenue, The, 135
Between Your Sheets, 155
Birthday, A, 72
Body Language, 110
Bungler, The, 221
Carrefour, 50
Caution, The, 247
China, 272
Chloe and Myra (extract from), 230
Clio (extract from), 244
Coat, 105
Colder, 252
Comment, 57
Configurations, 273
Connoisseuse of Slugs, The, 133
Conviction (iv), 265
Courtship, The, 12
Cupid Lost, 78
Dead Love, 197
Disappointed Wife, The, 170
Disappointment, The, 128
Do Not Make Things Too Easy, 189
Do You Not Know That I Need To Touch You, 279
Double Bed, 168

Douglas, Douglas, Tender and True, 142
Echo, 150
Encounter, 202
Ettrick, 238
Evadne, 269
Eve-Song, 164
Faithful Wife, The, 90
Fall, The, 196
Farmer's Bride, The, 82
Feather, The, 194
Felix Holt, The Radical (extracts from), 219, 253
Finale, 109
Fired Pot, The, 261
Fire Us With Ice, Burn Us With Snow, 121
First Farewell to J.G., 98
First Love, 3
Flight, The, 206
Forsaken Wife, The, 92
Freddy, 240
Freedom, 104
Friendship After Love, 280
From The Telephone, 113
From The Garden, 116
Gift, The, 99
Gifts, 228
Giving, 43
Hail, Blushing Goddess, Beauteous Spring! 264
Happy Ending, 199
Hares, The, 200
He Fumbles at Your Soul, 268
He That None Can Capture, 276
Heart and Mind, 60
Hesitate to Call, 95
Hickie, The, 257
Honeymoon Is Over, The, 89
How Lisa Loved the King (extract from), 23
Humble Wish, The, 165
Hymn to Eros, 120
'I Am Beset With a Dream of Fair Woman', 177
I Grieve and Dare Not Show My Discontent, 24
I Made a House of Houselessness, 93
I Must Be Able to Protect You, 136
Infelice, 214
In Recompense, 205
In the Orchard, 210
Invitation, 13
I Remember, 67
IS/NOT, 191
I Want To Love You Very Much, 223

I Will Not Give Thee All My Heart, 161
I Would Live In Your Love, 66
Jealousy, 251
Kiss, The, 138
Kiss'd Yestreen, 286
Last Testaments (extract from), 145
Letter to Daphnis, A, 232
Letter to her Husband, Absent Upon Publick Employment, A, 226
Letter to Miss E.B. on Marriage (extract from), 86
Letter, The, 48
Lines, Written on Seeing My Husband's Picture, 30
Look, The, 101
Love and Friendship, 198
Love Arm'd, 248
Love Letter, 74
Love Me At Last, 55
Love's Advocate, 146
Love Song, 15
love u.s.a., 182
Love's Witness, 1
Love-poem, 140
Lover: A Ballad, The, 162
Loving you, 137
Lynmouth Widow, A, 141
Man In Love, A, 156
Many and More, 278
Marriage, 84
Mary's Song, 157
Meeting, The, 224
Midcentury Love Letter, 14
Moment, A, 100
More and more, 267
Mortal Lease, The, 10
My Dearest Dust, 237
My Life Closed Twice, 227
My Mouth Hovers Across Your Breasts, 181
'My True Love Hath My Heart', 233
Narcissus, 111
Night-piece, 270
No, Go On, 96
Not-Loving, 262
Now I Have Nothing, 94
O Donald! Ye Are Just the Man, 166
Of Earthly Love, 64
Oh, How the Hand the Lover Ought to Prize, 139
Old Man, The, 134
Once We Played, 42
One Flesh, 284
On Jealousy, 250

On Loving Once and Loving Often, 91
On Monsieur's Departure, 24
On the Death of Mrs. Bowes, 88
On the Threshold, 220
Open Secrets, 117
Oppenheim's Cup and Saucer, 178
Other Woman, The, 256
Parable of the Four-Poster, 186
Paradox, 190
Passion (extract from), 124
Pastoral Dialogue, 76
Perfect Timing, 8
Petition, A, 255
Poem for Sigmund, 132
Prayer for Indifference, A (extract from), 25
Prophetic Soul, 123
Quest, The, 70
Remedia Amoris, 56
Remember, 149
Renouncement, 44
Request of Alexis, The, 54
Sea Love, 195
'Sea's Wash in the Hollow of the Heart . . . , The', 62
Second Thoughts, 179
Secret Flowers, 61
Semi-skilled Lover, 243
Siena, 52
Silent Is The House (extract from), 184
Siller Croun, The, 143
Slighted Lady, The, 32
Social Note, 35
Solitude, 174
So Long, 266
Song [Behn], 68
Song [Chudleigh], 154
Song [Du Bois], 6
Song [Fraser], 176
Song [Manley], 249
Song [Taylor], 37
Song [Wharton], 215
Song [Wilmot], 160
Song [Wroth], 80
Song, A [Finch], 69
Song, A [Pilkington], 103
Song of Obstacles, 9
Song of the Fucked Duck, 217
Sonnet [Richardson], 47
Sonnet [Rossetti], 2
Sonnet for Christmas, 283

Sonnet from the Portuguese V, 188
Sonnet from the Portuguese VI, 46
Sonnet from the Portuguese XIV, 231
Sonnet from the Portuguese XXII, 17
Sonnet from the Portuguese XXXVIII, 11
Sonnet from the Portuguese XLIII, 185
Sonnet II [Millay], 97
Sonnet X [Millay], 59
Sonnet XLI [Millay], 106
So This Is Love, 281
Sous-entendu, 241
Spilt Milk, 258
Spinster, 108
Stanzas, 4
Stocking Up, 282
Storm, The, 222
Story of a Hotel Room, 259
Sympathy, 235
Symphony Recital, 260
Taxi, The, 225
Thinking of Love, 263
Those Who Love, 144
Thread, 234
Tides, 218
'Tis Customary As We Part, 209
To a Lady Making Love, 39
To Alexis in Answer to his Poem against Fruition, 38
To Colindra, 212
To Cupid, 79
To J.G. on the News of his Marriage, 36
To Lysander, 102
To My Dear and Loving Husband, 29
To My Excellent Lucasia, On Our Friendship, 180
To My Heavenly Charmer, 122
To My Husband, 148
To My Rival, 254
To My Young Lover, 58
To One Persuading a Lady to Marriage, 242
To One That Asked Me Why I Lov'd J.G., 18
To Speak Of My Influences, 118
Touch Wood, 65
Truce, The, 71
Two Songs, 126
Two Truths, 85
Unfortunate Coincidence, 115
Unfortunate Damsel, The, 22
Uphold Me, 63
Upon the Death of her Husband (extract from), 151
Urania (extract from ), 277

Vain Advice, The, 51
Valentine, A (extract from), 77
Variations on the Word Love, 20
Verses Written on her Death-bed at Bath to her Husband in London, 236
Vicious Circle, 246
Villeggiature, 114
Vision, 73
Way of It, The, 216
We Who Have Loved, 201
Werena My Heart Licht I Wad Dee, 152
When I Was Fair and Young, 187
When Last We Parted, 204
Why Do I Love You, Sir? 19
Why? 53
Willing Mistriss, The, 274
Wine Is Drunk, The, 192
Winter, 147
Wish, The, 28
Women, 175
Women Are Different . . . , 41
Worth Dying For, 208
Wrestling, 16
Youth and Maidenhood (extract from), 159

# INDEX OF FIRST LINES

A fist of red fire, a flower, 3
After the fierce midsummer all ablaze, 280
After they had not made love, 199
Ah, Dangerous Swain, tell me no more, 249
Ah, gaze not on those eyes! forbear, 51
Ah me, if I grew sweet to man, 158
All my life I have struggled from gentleness, 109
A man and woman walking, 194
*Amyntas* led me to a Grove, 274
And auld Robin Forbes hes gien tem a dance, 239
And still my feelings sprout richest, 63
And ye shall walk in silk attire, 143
A Scholar first my Love implor'd, 6
As *Corydon* went shiv'ring by, 121
As loving Hind that (Hartless) wants her Deer, 226
At length, by so much importunity pressed, 162
Because she wants to touch him, 186
Because you are beautiful I will have to tell you a number of my secrets, 117
Because your eyes are slant and slow, 123
Before she walked into the river, 145
Beloved, thou has brought me many flowers, 185
Between your sheets you soundly sleep, 155
Blindfold I should to Myra run, 230
But lovers are like umbrellas, arnt they? 193
By the first of August, 67
By the time you swear you're his, 115
Child, with many a childish wile, 79
Come to me in the silence of the night, 150
Come, dark-eyed Sleep, thou child of Night, 5
Come, my beloved, 116
Come, the wind may never again, 184
Could you come back to me, Douglas, Douglas, 142
Daphnis dearest, wherefore weave me, 213
'Darling,' he said, 'I never meant, 85
Did I boast of liberty? 277
Do not make things too easy, 189
Do you not know that I need to touch you, 279
Don't think, 241
Down poured the rain; the closed window streamed, 222
Farewell my dearer half, joy of my heart, 98
First form your artful looks with studious care, 40
First time he kissed me, he but only kissed, 11
For I have read, 64
Forbear, bold Youth; all's Heaven here, 242
For some years he still would harden as he, 196

For years he's gone over her parting words, 96
From behind he looks like a man, 272
Give, give me back that Trifle you despise, 54
Go from me. Yet I feel that I shall stand, 46
Good madam, when ladies are willing, 39
Had I remained in innocent security, 245
Hail, blushing goddess, beauteous Spring! 264
Hail, happy bride, for thou art truly blest! 88
He draws memory out of me with hands of fire, 124
He fumbles at your Soul, 268
He gives her all the configurations, 273
He loved her so he wrote, 110
He nice frum far, but far frum nice, 246
He that none can capture, 276
He told his life story to Mrs. Courtly, 285
He was straight and strong, and his eyes were blue, 141
High, hollowed in green, 70
His pains so racked my heart, 235
Honour, that Guardian Angel, can alone, 244
How can I write about you, 233
How hardly I concealed my tears, 215
I am away from home, 90
I am beset with a dream of fair woman, 177
I am curiously stirred, 12
I ask no kind return in love, 25
I ask not wit, nor beauty do I crave, 165
I, being born a woman and distressed, 106
I did not live until this time, 180
I do not like my state of mind, 260
If ever two were one, then surely we, 29
I first tasted under Apollo's lips, 269
If I love you, 234
If thou must love me, let it be for nought, 231
If we shall live, we live, 208
I grieve and dare not show my discontent, 24
I lift my heavy heart up solemnly, 188
I like to get off with people, 265
I love you, Mrs. Acorn. Would your husband mind, 176
I made a house of houselessness, 93
Immobile, but fearless, 200
I mouth, 257
I must be able to protect you, 136
I must not think of thee; and, tired yet strong, 44
Incautious *Youth*, why do'st thou so mis-place, 58
In our town, people live in rows, 261
In using there are always two, 217
I remember sitting together in parks, 146
I saw our golden years on a black gale, 283
Is it to me, this sad lamenting strain? 34

Is love a light for me? A steady light, 61
I sowed the seeds of love, 22
I span and Eve span, 164
I still shall smile and go my careless way, 47
I take my pen in hand, 48
I thought of leaving her for a day, 179
"I thought you loved me." "No, it was only fun", 210
It's a funny thing, 132
I wad ha'e gi'en him my lips tae kiss, 157
I want to love you very much, 223
I will not give thee all my heart, 161
I wish I could remember that first day, 2
I would live in your love as the sea-grasses live in the sea, 66
I write in praise of the solitary act, 107
Kiss'd yestreen, and kiss'd yestreen, 286
Lad, come kiss me, 13
Lady, lady should you meet, 35
Lady, whom  my belovéd loves so well, 255
Late in the Forest I did Cupid See, 78
Like a drop of water is my heart, 159
Lived to see you throwing, 95
Look back with longing eyes and know that I will follow, 206
Love, a child, is ever crying, 80
*Love*, and the *Gout* invade the idle *Brain*, 56
Love in fantastic triumph sate, 248
love in the peaceful u.s.a., 182
Love is like the wild rose-briar, 198
Love is not a profession, 191
Love me at last, or if you will not, 55
Love, thou are best of Human Joys, 69
Love? We should smother it, 81
*Love* without *Hope* is like *Breath* without *Air*, 212
Lying apart now, each in a separate bed, 284
Mankind should hope, in wedlock's state, 86
Methinks, 'tis strange you can't afford, 92
More and more frequently the edges, 267
My brain burns with hate of you, 190
My dearest dust, could not thy hasty day, 237
My heart is like a singing bird, 72
My life closed twice before its close, 227
My Love? alas! I must not call you Mine, 36
My man loved me so much, 266
My mouth hovers across your breasts, 181
My poor expecting Heart beats for thy Breast, 122
My window, framed in pear-tree bloom, 114
Nobody knows what I feel about Freddy, 240
No more alone sleeping, no more alone waking, 84
Not easy to state the change you made, 74
Not that I cared about the other women, 252

Nothing ades to Loves fond fire, 160
Nothing like her ever came his way before, 243
Now for the long years when I could not love you, 205
Now heaven be thanked. I am out of love again! 104
Now I am glad to be one whom people ignore, 112
Now I have nothing. Even the joy of loss, 94
Now this particular girl, 108
O Donald! ye are just the man, 166
O Eros, silently smiling one, hear me, 120
O god, my dream! I dreamed that you were dead, 220
O Love! that stronger art than wine, 68
O patient shore, that canst not go to meet, 218
O shield me from his rage, celestial Powers! 250
O you, 50
Often after we make love, 134
Oh never weep for love that's dead, 197
Oh, come to me in dreams, my love! 4
Oh, how the hand the lover ought to prize, 139
Oh, life is a glorious cycle of song, 57
Oh, my beloved, have you thought of this, 59
Once loving is a gen'ral Fashion, 91
Once we played at love together, 42
One day the Amorous *Lysander*, 128
Our oneness is the wrestlers', fierce and close, 16
Out of the dark cup, 113
Remember me when I am gone away, 149
Remember when you love, from that same hour, 76
Said the Lion to the Lioness - 'When you are amber dust, 60
Sex, as they harshly call it, 126
She asked me to luncheon in fur. Far from, 178
She chooses her clothes in subdued colours, 256
She goes upstairs early, 168
She watched all day that she might see him pass, 23
Since man with that inconstancy was born, 38
Since we through war awhile must part, 229
Since you dare Brave me, with a Rivals Name, 254
Slight unpremeditated Words are borne, 1
So this is love, a kind of sad dance, 281
soft as old silk, 137
Soft kisses may be innocent, 247
Sometimes I have wanted, 105
Stay near me. Speak my name. Oh, do not wander, 14
Strephon hath Fashion, Wit and Youth, 37
Strephon kissed me in the spring, 101
Strephon, your breach of faith and trust, 103
Take back the heart you with such caution give, 102
*That* desire is quite over, 263
The ardent lover cannot find, 170
The bloom on the fruit is perfect, 207

The clouds had made a crimson crown, 100
The honeymoon is over, 89
The man who feels the dear disease, 156
The man with the big mouth, 275
The meadow and the mountain with desire, 125
The moon has fallen on her back, 270
The myrtle bush grew shady, 251
The night I fell in love with you I lost my watch, 8
the room contains no sound, 45
The snow is white on wood and wold, 138
The spine doesn't give or arch to it, 262
The tree still bends over the lake, 147
The wine is drunk, the woman known, 192
There are many and more, 278
There is a strong wall about me to protect me, 15
There is a truce . . . O lovers, tell, 71
There is the loneliness of peopled places, 174
There was a man who won a beautiful woman, 32
There was ance a may, and she lo'ed na men, 152
Thinking we were safe - insanity! 259
This is a word we use to plug, 20
This is the way o it, wide world over, 216
This man's metallic; at a sudden blow, 253
This to the crown and blessing of my life, 232
Those are the features, those the smiles, 30
Those who love the most, 144
Thou who dost all my worldly thoughts employ, 236
Three Summers since I chose a maid, 82
Tide be runnin' the great world over, 195
Time does not bring relief; you all have lied, 97
'Tis customary as we part, 209
To-day there have been lovely things, 73
To speak of my influences, 118
Touch wood, be humble, never dare to say, 65
Turn from that road's beguiling ease; return, 62
Two soluble aspirins spore in this glass, their mycelia, 258
Walking swiftly with a dreadful duchess, 214
We come now to the space which is boy-shaped, 7
We made our high bed in the low chapel, 271
We meet again, 202
We started speaking, 224
We who have loved, alas! may not be friends, 201
What can I give you, my lord, my lover, 99
What he liked in her voice, 111
When from the world, I shall be tane, 148
When I go away from you, 225
When I was a connoisseuse of slugs, 133
When I was fair and young, then favour graced me, 187
When last we parted, thou wert young and fair, 204

When my lover touches me, what I feel in my body, 9
When our two souls stand up erect and strong, 17
When the sheep are in the fauld, and the kye at hame, 26
When to Love's influence woman yields, 77
When we first rade down Ettrick, 238
When you gain her Affection, take care to preserve it, 167
Whilst thou art far away, I am at peace, 52
Who has not seen their lover, 135
Why *Damon*, why, why, why so pressing? 154
Why did you come, with your enkindled eyes, 53
Why do I love? Go, ask the Glorious Sun, 18
'Why do I love' You, Sir? 19
Why, there are maidens of heroic touch, 219
Winter shall not find me withered, 282
women, 175
Would but indulgent Fortune send, 28
Yet for one rounded moment I will be, 10
Yet, gentle shade! whether thou now dost rove, 151
You ask me what since we must part, 228
You dare not let your eyes meet theirs, 41
You glow in my heart, 221
You think I give myself to you? 43
Yours is the face that the earth turns to me, 140

# ACKNOWLEDGEMENTS

The publishers and editor gratefully acknowledge the following for their permission to reprint copyright material:

'Against Coupling' and 'Happy Ending' from *Selected Poems* by Fleur Adcock (1983), © Fleur Adcock 1983, reprinted by permission of Oxford University Press; 'Many and more' from *I Shall Not Be Moved* by Maya Angelou (1990), reprinted by permission of Random House Inc., and Virago Press, copyright © Maya Angelou 1990; 'Mary's Song' from *The Turn of the Day* by Marion Angus reprinted by permission of Faber and Faber Ltd; 'More and more' © Margaret Atwood 1968 (from *Margaret Atwood Poems 1965-1975*, Virago), 'Variations on the word love' © Margaret Atwood 1981 (from *True Stories*, Cape), 'Is/Not' © Margaret Atwood 1974 (from *Margaret Atwood Poems 1965-1975*, Virago) reprinted by permission of Curtis Brown Ltd London; 'The Faithful Wife' from *Collected Poems* by Patricia Beer (1988) reprinted by permission of Carcanet Press Ltd © Patricia Beer; 'The Courtship' from *Songs a Thracian Taught Me* (1980) reprinted by permission of Marion Boyars Publishers London and New York © Ann Beresford; 'The Feather' from *Collected Poems* by Lilian Bowes Lyon published by Jonathan Cape, reprinted by permission of Random House and the Literary Executors of the Lilian Bowes Lyon Estate; 'At 3 a.m.' from *Making Cocoa for Kingsley Amis*, reprinted by permission of Faber and Faber Ltd © Wendy Cope; 'So Long' from *Coagulations: New and Selected Poems* by Jayne Cortez published by Pluto Press, 1984, copyright © Jayne Cortez; 'Poem for Sigmund', 'So This Is Love' and extract from 'Last Testaments' from *Angels of Flesh Angels of Silence* reprinted by permission of the Canadian Publishers, McClelland & Stewart, Toronto, copyright © Lorna Crozier 1988; 'Thread' from *White Boats* by Catherine Lucy Czerkawska published by Akros Publications © Catherine Lucy Czerkawska 1976; 'At Sixteen' by Ann Darr, originally published in *Poetry Now*, © Ann Darr 1981 and reprinted with the poet's permission; all poems by Emily Dickinson reprinted by permission of the publishers and the Trustees of Amherst College, from *The Poems of Emily Dickinson*, edited by Thomas H. Johnson. The Belknap Press of Harvard University Press, Cambridge, Mass., copyright © 1951, 1955, 1983 by the President and Fellows of Harvard College. Also by permission of Little, Brown and Co. Copyright 1929 by Martha Dickinson Bianchi; 'No Go On' and 'At Les Deux Magots' from *Explaining Magnetism* by Maura Dooley (Bloodaxe Books, 1991) reprinted by permission of Bloodaxe Books Ltd; 'Evadne' from *Collected Poems* (ed. Louis L. Martz, 1984) by H.D. [Hilda Doolittle], reprinted by permission of Carcanet Press Limited and New Directions Publishing Corporation, copyright © 1982 by the Estate of Hilda Doolittle; 'Oppenheim's Cup and Saucer' from *Carol Ann Duffy: Standing Female Nude* (Anvil Press Poetry, 1985), reprinted by permission of